Arthur Henry Bullen

Lyrics from the Dramatists of the Elizabethan Age

Arthur Henry Bullen

Lyrics from the Dramatists of the Elizabethan Age

ISBN/EAN: 9783744768337

Printed in Europe, USA, Canada, Australia, Japan

Cover: Foto ©Thomas Meinert / pixelio.de

More available books at **www.hansebooks.com**

LYRICS
FROM THE DRAMATISTS OF THE ELIZABETHAN AGE.

NOTE.—*Five hundred and twenty copies of this edition printed for England and America, each of which is numbered as issued.*

No. 430.

LYRICS

FROM THE DRAMATISTS OF THE

ELIZABETHAN AGE:

EDITED BY

A. H. BULLEN.

LONDON:
JOHN C. NIMMO,
14, KING WILLIAM STREET, STRAND.
1889.

CHISWICK PRESS :—C. WHITTINGHAM AND CO., TOOKS COURT,
CHANCERY LANE.

INTRODUCTION.

THE scattered lyrical poetry of the Elizabethan age is as voluminous as it is excellent. I attempted to collect a portion of it in an anthology entitled *Lyrics from Elizabethan Song-books;* and I now add another chapter to the story. It is only by a patient and minute examination that we gradually become aware of the extent and wealth of this fruitful tract of English literature; if we advance too rapidly our survey must needs be defective. In the present volume I have gathered together the lyrics dispersed among the plays, masques, and pageants of the Elizabethan age,— allowing myself the usual privilege of construing the word "Elizabethan" in an elastic sense, so as to include all who "trafficked with the stage" in the days of James I. and Charles I. I advance from Lyly and Peele to Shirley and Sir William Davenant.[1]

[1] The ground had been traversed before by the late Robert Bell in his *Songs from the Dramatists*. My predecessor's labour covered a wider area than mine, Sheridan being the last name in his anthology. My collection, within the limits

It will be noticed that, though I have called this anthology *Lyrics from the Dramatists of the Elizabethan Age*, some dramatists are not represented. The most notable absentee is Robert Greene, whose lyrical poetry is of singular beauty. His exclusion is due to the fact that his lyrics are only found in his romances, not in his plays. Thomas Lodge stands in the same position. Both will be fully represented hereafter in a volume of *Lyrics from Elizabethan Romances;* but I am now concerned solely with the drama.

Adopting chronological order, I give the first place to John Lyly, who (unlike Greene) plentifully garnished his comedies with songs, while he never struck a lyrical note in his romance, *Euphues*. We are indebted to Edward Blount, the enterprising publisher who in 1632 issued a collective edition of Lyly's plays, for the preservation of these songs. They were not included in the original editions of Lyly's plays. In those days publishers frequently omitted songs when they put plays to press.[1] Marston's plays, for instance, have come down without any of the songs, though the stage-directions show that songs were provided in abundance.[2] There

---

that I have prescribed to myself, is somewhat fuller than Bell's.

[1] The late Mr. Hain Friswell in 1867 excised all the poetry from his edition of Sidney's *Arcadia!*

[2] Yet I can hardly believe that these lost songs were by

is in Lyly's songs a fairy lightness that presents a most refreshing contrast to the pedantic finery of *Euphues*. Where shall we find a conceit more neatly turned than in those delightful verses, frequently imitated but never equalled, "Cupid and my Campaspe played"? It must be remembered that Lyly's songs were written at a time when our English lyrists were doubtfully feeling their way. Lodge and Breton frequently relapse into the tedious long-winded measures employed by the elder poets; and Greene's touch is not always sure. But there is no fault to be found with Lyly's songs. Would that he had devoted himself to song-writing instead of toiling at his ponderous romance! "Sing to Apollo, God of day," and "O Cupid, monarch over kings," are jewels that "from each facet flash a laugh at time."

Though Peele's plays have but a dusty antiquarian interest, his songs are as fresh as the flowers in May. He was a rogue and sharper, according to the traditional account; but the author of *The Arraignment of Paris* and of the noble song in *Polyhymnia* must surely have been a man of

Marston, and suspect that the players had to procure them from some other quarter. Where plays were represented by companies of boy-actors (as in the case of Lyly and Marston) songs were usually introduced, for the boys had been carefully trained in singing, and opportunities had to be afforded to them of displaying their accomplishment.

gentle and chivalrous character. The reader will not fail to notice the beauty of the lyrical snatches from *The Old Wives' Tale.* It is a pity that we possess only fragments of Peele's pastoral play, *The Hunting of Cupid*, which was licensed for the press in 1591.

Thomas Nashe, "ingenious, ingenuous, fluent, facetious T. Nashe," was very serious at times. Witness his *Christ's Tears over Jerusalem*, that woeful cry wrung from the depths of a passionate soul. The songs in *Summer's last Will and Testament* are of a sombre turn. We have, it is true, the delicious verses in praise of spring; and what a pleasure it is to croon them over!

> "The fields breathe sweet, the daisies kiss our feet,
> Young lovers meet, old wives a-sunning sit."

But when the play was produced it was sickly autumn, and the plague was stalking through the land:

> "Short days, sharp days, long nights come on apace:
> Ah, who shall hide us from the winter's face?
> Cold doth increase, the sickness will not cease,
> And here we lie, God knows, with little ease."

Very vividly does Nashe depict the feeling of forlorn hopelessness caused by the dolorous advent of the dreaded pestilence. His address to the fading summer, "Go not yet hence, bright soul of the sad year," is no empty rhetorical appeal, but a solemn supplication; and those pathetic stanzas, "Adieu; farewell, earth's bliss," must have had strange significance at a time when on every side the death-bells were tolling.

Shakespeare's songs are of course written "divinely well." Yet I must frankly confess that I cannot determine to my own satisfaction whether Shakespeare or Fletcher wrote the opening song, "Roses, their sharp spines being gone," in *The Two Noble Kinsmen*. Such a line as:

"Oxlips in their cradles growing"

would seem to be Shakespeare's very own. The text of the song has been somewhat corrupted. "Primrose ... with *her bells* dim" cannot be what the poet wrote, for primroses have no bells; and I am inclined to accept the emendation of that venerable poet, Mr. W. J. Linton, "with harebell slim."

With all my admiration for Ben Jonson, I venture to think that his lyrics—excellent as they frequently are—want the natural magic that we find in the songs of some of his less famous contemporaries. "Still to be neat, still to be drest," and others, are polished *ad unguem*, so that the severest critic cannot discover a flaw. And who can fail to appreciate the fertility of invention that Jonson displays in his masques? Few, indeed, are the poets who have so happily combined learning, smoothness, and sprightliness. He has mingled

> "all the sweets and salts
> That none may say the triumph halts."

His lyrical work has frequently a pronounced epigrammatic flavour. We admire the compactness of thought and the aptness of expression; we exclaim "Euge, euge!" and are ready to affirm that Martial at his smartest cannot compare with rare Ben Jonson. Yet somehow the wayward inspiration of poets who have no claim to be Jonson's peers is more powerfully attractive.

Ben's antagonist, Dekker, had a genuine lyrical gift. His life was one constant strenuous struggle with poverty, and all his work was done in haste and hurry. He was not unfrequently lodged in the Counter (a prison in the Poultry for debtors), where it was difficult to write with any comfort or satisfaction. But in the dusk and gloom his cheeriness never forsook him; his songs—too few, alas!—are blithe as the lark's tirra-lirra and wholesome as the breath of June.

Francis Beaumont and John Fletcher were lyrists of the first rank. In his *Inner Temple Masque* Beaumont gave ample proof of his ability for song-writing. What a rapture is in this call to the masquers to begin the dance!

> "Shake off your heavy trance!
> And leap into a dance
> Such as no mortals use to tread:
> Fit only for Apollo
> To play to, for the moon to lead,
> And all the stars to follow!"

Of rare beauty are the glowing and tender bridal songs in this masque; and I would certainly ascribe to Beaumont the bridal songs in *The Maid's Tragedy*. That admirable burlesque, *The Knight of the Burning Pestle*, is now regarded as mainly the work of Beaumont, and we may be fairly confident that it was he who wrote the whimsical song of Ralph the May-lord, "London, to thee I do present" (pp. 92-4). But the largest contributor to our anthology is Beaumont's coadjutor, John Fletcher. I have drawn copiously from *The Faithful Shepherdess*, the best of English pastoral plays. It is deeply to be regretted that Fletcher by the introduction of offensive matter smirched the fair features of a poem that would otherwise be at all points delightful. The rhymed trochaics glide as lightly as the satyr who bore the sleeping Alexis to Clorin's bower. At its original representation *The Faithful Shepherdess* failed to please; but it came from the press crowned with the praises of Beaumont, Ben Jonson, Nat Field, and Chapman.

The finest compliment was paid by Chapman, who declared that the poem

> "Renews the golden world, and holds through all
> The holy laws of homely pastoral,
> Where flowers and founts, and nymphs and semi-gods,
> And all the Graces find their old abodes."

Milton's *Comus* owes not a little to Fletcher's pastoral; and *Il Penseroso* is under obligations to that fine song in *Nice Valour*, "Hence, all you vain delights!" Some of the best of Fletcher's songs are in *Valentinian*, where we have the rousing address to "God Lyæus, ever young" (worthy to stand beside Shakespeare's "Come, thou monarch of the vine,") and that softest of invocations to "Care-charming Sleep."

Massinger, an admirable dramatist, had little lyrical power—in fact, none at all—for his few attempts at a song are flat and insipid. Ford's songs are of small account, and Marston was no songbird. Webster has three lyrical passages of deep impressiveness—the dirge in *The White Devil* ("Call for the robin-redbreast and the wren"), the passing-song in *The Duchess of Malfi* ("Hark, now everything is still"), and the *memento mori* in *The Devil's Law-Case* ("All the flowers of the spring").

Thomas Heywood[1] wrote some very pleasant

---

[1] Some of the songs in Heywood's plays are by other hands. For instance, in *The Rape of Lucrece* he introduces two stanzas of Sir Walter Raleigh's little poem, "Now what

songs, notably the fresh matin-song, "Pack, clouds, away, and welcome, day!" (which Sir Henry Bishop set to music), and the tuneful love-greeting to Phillis, "Ye little birds that sit and sing." The hymns to Dian and Ceres in *The Golden Age* and *Silver Age*, and the address to Phœbus in *Love's Mistress*, are graceful and melodious. I have not included Heywood's jocular songs; some are amusing, but others are not strictly decorous.

William Rowley, whose blank verse is so awkward, could gambol nimbly in rhyme. From his odd play, *The Thracian Wonder*, I have quoted several songs, perhaps too many; but I am not sure that he wrote them all. The rollicking songs in *The Spanish Gipsy* I take to be by Rowley rather than by his *collaborateur* Middleton. In *More Dissemblers besides Women* we have some gipsy songs, evidently from the hand that contri-

is love? I pray thee tell." In *Edward IV.* we have one stanza from an old ballad of Agincourt :—

> "Agincourt, Agincourt ! know ye not Agincourt,
> Where the English slew and hurt
> All the French foemen ?
> With our guns and bills brown,
> O, the French were beaten down,
> Morris-pikes and bowmen."

The complete ballad, in eleven stanzas, may be seen in J. P. Collier's privately-printed collection of *Broadside Black-letter Ballads*, 1868.

buted the songs to *The Spanish Gipsy*. *More Dissemblers* is ascribed in the old edition (posthumously published in 1657) solely to Middleton, but I have no doubt that Rowley had a hand in it. Middleton's best lyrical work, highly fantastic and picturesque, is seen in *The Witch*.

Shirley's songs remind us sometimes of Fletcher, sometimes of Ben Jonson. He was of an imitative turn, and followed his models closely; but in his most famous song, "The glories of our blood and state," and in those equally memorable stanzas, "Victorious men of earth, no more," he struck an original note, deep-toned and solemn.

Suckling's gaiety is very enlivening. His "Why so pale and wan, fond lover?" is a triumph of playful raillery; and hardly inferior is the toast, "Here's a health to the nutbrown lass!" which Sheridan imitated in "Here's to the maiden of bashful fifteen." Occasionally, in his more serious moods, Suckling follows the lead of Donne, and elaborates subtle conceits. "No, no, fair heretic, it needs must be," might readily pass as the work of Donne, who exercised a potent influence on his younger contemporaries.

Randolph's plays yield only some bacchanalian snatches; Cartwright wrote a few good songs, but the best are too free for our anthology; Habington, whose poems to Castara are often so painfully modest as to become insipid, has one capital song in *The Queen of Arragon*—a flouting address to a proud mistress; Peter Hausted's *Rival Friends* has several good songs; Aurelian Townshend, "the poor poet of the Barbican," contributes some smooth verses from his masque, *Albion's Triumph;* and Francis Quarles, famed for his *Emblems*, has a little song (wrongfully claimed for Richard Brome) in praise of solitude. That witty divine, Jasper Mayne, who suffered at the hands of Cromwell, but became Canon of Christ Church and Archdeacon of Chichester at the Restoration, wrote two very readable comedies. In one of them, *The Amorous War*, is found the song, "Time is the feathered thing," of intricate metrical construction and somewhat harshly worded, but rich and weighty. Another canon of Christ Church, Dr. William Strode, was something of a poet; his academic play, *The Floating Island*, supplies one short song. At this time divines were much addicted to the writing of plays. In Dr. Jasper Fisher's *Fuimus Troes*, acted at Magdalen College, Oxford, in 1633, there are several songs, but they are not of the best quality. Samuel Harding, of Exeter College, who became chaplain to a nobleman and died during the Civil Wars, published in 1640 a play, *Sicily and Naples, or The Fatal Union*, from which I have drawn those quaint grim verses, "Noblest bodies are but gilded clay." A certain John Jones (of whom nothing is known), in his play, *Adrasta*, 1635,

has a good dirge, beginning "Die, die, ah die!"
Our old poets were fond of dirges and of bridal
songs. Joseph Rutter, in *The Shepherd's Holiday*,
has some graceful verses in praise of "Hymen, god
of marriage-bed" (p. 206); and Nathaniel Field
at an earlier date (p. 175) had celebrated the ad-
vantages of the marriage-state. In Cartwright's
Ordinary there is a good epithalamium, and another
may be seen in Robert Chamberlain's *Swaggering
Damsels;* but as these poets did not observe the
reticence which modern taste demands, I have
excluded their sportive effusions.

Milton is represented by extracts from *Arcades*
and *Comus*. Master of all the learning of all the
ages, Milton had not neglected to read and digest
the writings of the Elizabethan poets. He borrowed
freely from any and every source, turning whatever
he touched to pure gold. Warton's discursive
annotations to Milton's minor poems are a peren-
nial feast.

Sir William Davenant began to write when many
of the Elizabethan poets were still at work, and he
caught something of their inspiration. In his
songs there are sprightly runnings of the generous
fancy that brimmed in the lyrics of Fletcher; but
he belongs rather to the Restoration than to the
earlier age. He may have shaken hands with
Dekker, but Dryden was his familiar friend. He
stands as a sort of half-way house between the

Elizabethans and the Restoration; and he offers very fair entertainment to passing travellers.

I have mentioned many of the contributors to our anthology, but the list is not exhausted. Some fresh-coloured verses in praise of Robin Hood (p. 87) are from a rare pageant of Anthony Munday, who also wrote Robin's Dirge (p. 86). Thomas Goffe has several good songs; and Richard Brome is not forgotten. Among the masque-writers represented are Samuel Daniel, Dr. Campion, and William Browne; and I have drawn from some anonymous masques. If any songs of merit have escaped my notice I will endeavour to repair the fault hereafter; but I have been at some pains to make the collection as complete as possible.

INDEX OF FIRST LINES.

INDEX OF FIRST LINES.

	PAGE
A CURSE upon thee for a slave (*John Fletcher*)	134
Adieu; farewell earth's bliss (*Nashe*)	25
All that glisters is not gold (*Shakespeare*)	37
All the flowers of the spring (*Webster*)	143
All ye that lovely lovers be (*Peele*)	19
All ye woods, and trees, and bowers (*John Fletcher*)	111
Among all sorts of people (*Shirley*)	181
And will he not come again (*Shakespeare*)	49
Are they shadows that we see? (*Daniel*)	75
Arm, arm, arm, arm! the scouts are all come in (*John Fletcher*)	121
Art thou god to shepherd turned (*Shakespeare*)	46
Art thou gone in haste (*William Rowley*)	152
Art thou poor, yet hast thou golden slumbers (*Dekker*)	80
At Venus' entreaty for Cupid her son (*Peele*)	18
Autumn hath all the Summer's fruitful treasure (*Nashe*)	24
Away, delights! go seek some other dwelling (*John Fletcher*)	114
Beauty, alas! where wast thou born (*Lodge and Greene*)	21
Beauty, arise, show forth thy glorious shining (*Dekker*)	81
Beauty clear and fair (*John Fletcher*)	138
Black spirits and white, red spirits and gray (*Middleton*)	166
Blow, blow, thou winter wind (*Shakespeare*)	44
Brave iron, brave hammer, from your sound (*Dekker*)	85
Buzz! quoth the Blue-Fly (*Ben Jonson*)	68
Call for the robin-redbreast and the wren (*Webster*)	142
Care-charming Sleep, thou easer of all woes (*John Fletcher*)	118
Cast away care! he that loves sorrow (*Dekker*)	84
Cast our caps and cares away (*John Fletcher*)	127
Cold's the wind, and wet's the rain (*Dekker*)	78
Cold Winter brings to crown your age (*Corona Minervæ*)	203
Come away, away, away! (*Shirley*)	182
Come away, bring on the bride (*John Fletcher*)	126

INDEX OF FIRST LINES.

	PAGE
Come away, come away (*Middleton*)	165
Come away, come away, Death (*Shakespeare*)	41
Come, come away! the spring (*Richard Brome*)	211
Come, follow me, you country lasses (*Fletcher and Rowley*)	139
Come, follow your leader, follow (*Middleton and Rowley*)	160
Come hither, you that love, and hear me sing (*John Fletcher*)	115
Come let the state stay (*Suckling*)	193
Come, lovers, bring your cares (*Jones*)	207
Come, lovely Boy! unto my court (*Rutter*)	205
Come, my Celia, let us prove (*Ben Jonson*)	62
Come, my children, let your feet (*Beaumont and Fletcher*)	95
Come, my dainty doxies (*Middleton?*)	168
Come, my Daphne, come away (*Shirley*)	185
Come, my sweet, whiles every strain (*Cartwright*)	194
Come, noble nymphs, and do not hide (*Ben Jonson*)	71
Come, shepherds, come (*John Fletcher*)	104
Come, shepherds, come, impale your brows (*Goffe*)	199
Come, Sleep, and with thy sweet deceiving (*Beaumont and Fletcher*)	90
Come, thou monarch of the vine (*Shakespeare*)	53
Come unto these yellow sands (*Shakespeare*)	55
Come, you whose loves are dead (*Beaumont and Fletcher*)	91
Comforts lasting, loves increasing (*John Ford*)	144
Cupid all his arts did prove (*Thomas Forde*)	230
Cupid and my Campaspe played (*Lyly*)	1
Cupid, if a god thou art (*Hausted*)	197
Cupid, pardon what is past (*Beaumont and Fletcher*)	97
Cynthia, to thy power and thee (*Beaumont and Fletcher*)	98
Dame, dame! the watch is set (*Ben Jonson*)	66
Dearest, do not you delay me (*John Fletcher*)	128
Did not the heavenly rhetoric of thine eye (*Shakespeare*)	30
Die, die, ah die (*Jones*)	207
Done to death by slanderous tongues (*Shakespeare*)	39
Drink to-day and drown all sorrow (*John Fletcher*)	137
Drop golden showers, gentle sleep (*Goffe*)	198
Drowsy Phœbus, come away (*Hausted*)	196
Eyes, hide my love and do not show (*Daniel*)	76
Fair and fair, and twice so fair (*Peele*)	13
Fair Apollo, whose bright beams (*William Rowley*)	157
Fair summer droops, droop men and beast therefore (*Nashe*)	23
Fear no more the heat of the sun (*Shakespeare*)	52
Fine young folly, though you were (*Habington*)	202

INDEX OF FIRST LINES.

	PAGE
Fly hence, shadows, that do keep (John Ford)	144
Fond Love, no more (Thomas Forde)	231
Foolish idle toys (William Rowley)	156
Fools, they are the only nation (Ben Jonson)	61
Fortune smiles, cry holiday! (Dekker)	79
From the east to western Ind (Shakespeare)	44
From thy forehead thus I take (John Fletcher)	105
Full fathom five thy father lies (Shakespeare)	56
Fy on sinful fantasy (Shakespeare)	40
Gently dip, but not too deep (Peele)	20
Go, happy heart! for thou shalt lie (John Fletcher)	119
God Lyæus, ever young (John Fletcher)	118
Golden slumbers kiss your eyes (Dekker)	81
Hail, beauteous Dian, queen of shades (Heywood)	147
Happy times we live to see (Middleton and Rowley)	158
Hark! hark! the lark at heaven's gate sings (Shakespeare)	51
Hark, now everything is still (Webster)	142
Hast thou seen the down in the air (Suckling)	193
Have pity, Grief; I cannot pay (Hausted)	197
Have you a desire to see (Hausted)	198
Haymakers, rakers, reapers and mowers (Dekker)	83
Hear, ye ladies that despise (John Fletcher)	117
Heigh-ho, what shall a shepherd do (Shirley)	186
Hence, all you vain delights (John Fletcher)	133
Hence with passion, sighs, and tears (Heywood)	148
Here lies the blithe spring (Dekker)	82
His golden locks Time hath to silver turned (Peele)	16
Hold back thy hours, dark Night, till we have done (Beaumont and Fletcher)	99
Hot sun, cool fire, tempered with sweet air (Peele)	20
How blest are they that waste their weary hours (Quarles)	195
How round the world goes, and every thing that's in it (Middleton)	167
How should I your true love know (Shakespeare)	49
Howsoe'er the minutes go (Heywood)	150
Hymen, god of marriage-bed (Rutter)	206
I care not for these idle toys (William Rowley)	152
I could never have the power (Beaumont and Fletcher)	100
I neither will lend or borrow (Shirley)	183
I was not wearier where I lay (Ben Jonson)	70
If I freely may discover (Ben Jonson)	59
If Love his arrows shoot so fast (Shirley)	180
If love make me forsworn, how shall I swear to love (Shakespeare)	28

	PAGE
If she be made of white and red (Shakespeare)	27
In a maiden-time professed (Middleton)	164
In Love's name you are charged hereby (Shirley)	179
In wet and cloudy mists I slowly rise (Luminalia)	208
Io, Bacchus! To thy table (Lyly)	11
Isis, the goddess of this land (John Fletcher)	124
It was a beauty that I saw (Ben Jonson)	74
It was a lover and his lass (Shakespeare)	47
Jog on, jog on, the footpath way (Shakespeare)	54
Lawn as white as driven snow (Shakespeare)	54
Lay a garland on my hearse (Beaumont and Fletcher)	100
Let the bells ring, and let the boys sing (John Fletcher)	129
Let those complain that feel Love's cruelty (John Fletcher)	131
Let us live, live! for, being dead (Davenant)	224
Live with me still, and all the measures (Dekker)	82
London, to thee I do present (Beaumont and Fletcher)	92
Love, a thousand sweets distilling (Shirley)	180
Love for such a cherry lip (Middleton)	162
Love is a law, a discord of such force (William Rowley)	151
Love is a sickness full of woes (Daniel)	76
Love is blind and a wanton (Ben Jonson)	60
Love is the sire, dam, nurse, and seed (Phineas Fletcher)	173
Love's a lovely lad (William Rowley)	154
Lovers, rejoice! your pains shall be rewarded (Beaumont and Fletcher)	96
Matilda, now go take thy bed (Davenport)	212
Melampus, when will love be void of fears? (Peele)	17
Melpomene, the muse of tragic songs (Peele)	15
My Daphne's hair is twisted gold (Lyly)	8
My shag-hair Cyclops, come, let's fly (Lyly)	4
No, no, fair heretic, it needs must be (Suckling)	192
Noblest bodies are but gilded clay (Harding)	209
Nor Love, nor Fate dare I accuse (Richard Brome)	210
Now does jolly Janus greet your merriment (William Rowley)	153
Now fie on love, it ill befits (Goffe?)	199
Now hath Flora robbed her bowers (Campion)	88
Now the hungry lion roars (Shakespeare)	35
Now the lusty spring is seen (John Fletcher)	116
Now wend we together, my merry men all (Munday)	87
Now while the moon doth rule the sky (John Fletcher)	107
Nymphs and shepherds, dance no more (Milton)	213

INDEX OF FIRST LINES.

	PAGE
O cruel Love, on thee I lay (*Lyly*)	3
O Cupid! monarch over kings (*Lyly*)	12
O fair sweet face! O eyes celestial bright (*John Fletcher*)	123
O fair sweet goddess! queen of loves (*John Fletcher*)	121
O fly, my soul! what hangs upon (*Shirley*)	185
O for a bowl of fat canary (*Middleton?*)	163
O gentle Love, ungentle for thy deed (*Peele*)	14
O, how my lungs do tickle! ha, ha, ha! (*John Fletcher*)	135
O mistress mine, where are you roaming? (*Shakespeare*)	41
O sorrow, sorrow, say where dost thou dwell? (*Samuel Rowley?*)	174
O stay, O turn, O pity me (*William Rowley*)	153
O that joy so soon should waste (*Ben Jonson*)	57
O the month of May, the merry month of May (*Dekker*)	77
O turn thy bow (*John Fletcher*)	132
O yes, O yes! if any maid (*Lyly*)	7
O'er the smooth enamelled green (*Milton*)	213
Of Pan we sing, the best of singers, Pan (*Ben Jonson*)	73
On a day—alack the day! (*Shakespeare*)	31
Once Venus' cheeks, that shamed the morn (*Strode*)	212
Orpheus I am, come from the depths below (*John Fletcher*)	120
Orpheus with his lute made trees (*John Fletcher?*)	141
Over hill, over dale (*Shakespeare*)	33
Pack, clouds, away, and welcome day (*Heywood*)	146
Pan's Syrinx was a girl indeed (*Lyly*)	9
Pardon, goddess of the night (*Shakespeare*)	40
Peace and silence be the guide (*Beaumont*)	90
Phœbus, unto thee we sing (*Heywood*)	149
Pinch him, pinch him, black and blue (*Lyly*)	6
Queen and huntress, chaste and fair (*Ben Jonson*)	58
Rise from the shades below (*John Fletcher*)	122
Rise, lady mistress, rise (*Nathaniel Field*)	175
Roses, their sharp spines being gone (*Shakespeare?*)	140
Run to love's lottery! Run, maids, and rejoice (*Davenant*)	221
Sabrina fair (*Milton*)	216
Seal up her eyes, O sleep, but flow (*Cartwright*)	195
See the chariot at hand here of Love (*Ben Jonson*)	68
Shake off your heavy trance (*Beaumont*)	89
She's pretty to walk with (*Suckling*)	192
Shepherds all, and maidens fair (*John Fletcher*)	104
Sigh no more, ladies, sigh no more (*Shakespeare*)	39
Since you desire my absence (*William Rowley*)	154

	PAGE
Sing his praises that doth keep (*John Fletcher*)	103
Sing to Apollo, god of day (*Lyly*)	10
Slaves are they that heap up mountains (*Randolph*)	190
Slow, slow, fresh fount, keep time with my salt tears (*Ben Jonson*)	57
So sweet a kiss the golden sun gives not (*Shakespeare*)	29
Spread, table, spread (*Peele*)	19
Spring all the Graces of the age (*Ben Jonson*)	70
Spring, the sweet Spring, is the year's pleasant king (*Nashe*)	22
Stand, who goes there? (*Lyly*)	5
Steer hither, steer your winged pines (*Browne*)	172
Still to be neat, still to be drest (*Ben Jonson*)	66
Still-born Silence, thou that art (*Flecknoe*)	220
Submit, bunch of grapes (*The London Chanticleers*)	200
Sweet Echo, sweetest nymph, that livest unseen (*Milton*)	216

Take, O, take those lips away (*Shakespeare*)	48
Tell me, dearest, what is Love? (*John Fletcher*)	113
Tell me, what is that only thing (*John Fletcher*)	123
Tell me where is fancy bred (*Shakespeare*)	37
The bread is all baked (*Davenant*)	225
The glories of our blood and state (*Shirley*)	189
The hour of sweety night decays apace (*The Mountebank's Masque*)	169
The nut-brown ale, the nut-brown (*Histriomastix*)	169
The ousel-cock so black of hue (*Shakespeare*)	34
The star that bids the shepherd fold (*Milton*)	214
Then, in a free and lofty strain (*Ben Jonson*)	61
Then is there mirth in heaven (*Shakespeare*)	48
There is not any wise man (*William Rowley*)	156
They that for worldly wealth do wed (*Nathaniel Field*)	175
This cursed jealousy, what is 't? (*Davenant*)	224
This way, this way, come and hear (*John Fletcher*)	127
Thou deity, swift-winged Love (*John Fletcher*)	132
Thou divinest, fairest, brightest (*John Fletcher*)	111
Thou more than most sweet glove (*Ben Jonson*)	58
Though I am young and cannot tell (*Ben Jonson*)	74
Though little be the god of love (*Shirley*)	187
Thrice the brinded cat hath mewed (*Shakespeare*)	50
Through yon same bending plain (*John Fletcher*)	101
Thus, thus begin the yearly rites (*Ben Jonson*)	72
Thy best hand lay on this turf of grass (*Rowley and Middleton*)	161
Time is the feathered thing (*Jasper Mayne*)	228
'Tis, in good truth, a most wonderful thing (*Davenant*)	223
'Tis late and cold; stir up the fire (*John Fletcher*)	130
'Tis mirth that fills the veins with blood (*Beaumont and Fletcher*)	91

INDEX OF FIRST LINES.

	PAGE
To bed, to bed! Come, Hymen, lead the bride (Beaumont and Fletcher)	99
To the Ocean now I fly (Milton)	219
Trip and go! heave and ho! (Nashe)	23
Trip it, gipsies, trip it fine (Middleton and Rowley)	158
Turn, turn thy beauteous face away (John Fletcher)	136
Under the greenwood tree (Shakespeare)	43
Up, youths and virgins! up, and praise (Ben Jonson)	63
Urns and odours bring away (John Fletcher!)	141
Victorious men of earth, no more (Shirley)	188
Wake all the dead! what ho! what ho! (Davenant)	227
Wake, our mirth begins to die (Ben Jonson)	60
Walking in a shadowed grove (Dabridgecourt Belchier)	170
We care not for money, riches or wealth (Randolph)	190
We that have known no greater state (Heywood)	150
Wedding is great Juno's crown (Shakespeare)	48
Weep eyes, break heart! (Middleton)	164
Weep no more for what is past (Davenant)	221
Weep no more, nor sigh, nor groan (John Fletcher)	137
Weep, weep, ye woodmen! wail (Munday)	86
Welcome, thrice welcome to this shady green (Massinger)	177
Welladay, welladay, poor Colin, thou art going to the ground (Peele)	15
What a dainty life the milkmaid leads (Nabbes)	201
What bird so sings, yet so does wail? (Lyly)	2
What makes me so unnimbly rise (Townshend)	204
What powerful charms my streams do bring (John Fletcher)	108
What thing is love? for, well I wot, love is a thing (Peele)	18
When daffodils begin to peer (Shakespeare)	53
When daisies pied and violets blue (Shakespeare)	31
When that I was and a little tiny boy (Shakespeare)	42
Whenas the rye reach to the chin (Peele)	19
Where did you borrow that last sigh (Berkley)	228
Where the bee sucks, there suck I (Shakespeare)	56
While you here do snoring lie (Shakespeare)	56
Whilst we sing the doleful knell (Swetnam, the Woman-Hater)	176
Whither shall I go (William Rowley)	155
Who is Silvia? what is she (Shakespeare)	27
Why art thou slow, thou rest of trouble, Death (Massinger)	177
Why should this a desert be (Shakespeare)	45
Why so pale and wan, fond lover (Suckling)	191

	PAGE
Will you buy any tape (*Shakespeare*)	55
With fair Ceres, Queen of Grain (*Heywood*)	148
Woodmen, shepherds, come away (*Shirley*)	178
Ye little birds that sit and sing (*Heywood*)	145
Ye should stay longer if we durst (*Beaumont*)	89
You spotted snakes with double tongue (*Shakespeare*)	34
You virgins, that did late despair (*Shirley*)	182

LYRICS FROM THE DRAMATISTS.

From JOHN LYLY'S *Alexander
and Campaspe*, 1584.[1]

CARDS AND KISSES.

CUPID and my Campaspe played
At cards for kisses—Cupid paid ;
He stakes his quiver, bow and arrows,
His mother's doves, and team of sparrows ;
Loses them too ; then down he throws
The coral of his lip, the rose
Growing on's cheek (but none knows how) ;
With these, the crystal of his brow,
And then the dimple of his chin :
All these did my Campaspe win.
At last he set her both his eyes,
She won, and Cupid blind did rise.
O Love ! has she done this to thee ?
What shall, alas ! become of me ?

[1] Lyly's songs are not found in the original editions of his plays. They first appeared in the collective edition of 1632.

SPRING'S WELCOME.

WHAT bird so sings, yet so does wail?
    O 'tis the ravished nightingale.
"Jug, jug, jug, jug, tereu," she cries,
And still her woes at midnight rise.
Brave prick-song![1] who is't now we hear?
None but the lark so shrill and clear;
Now at heaven's gates[2] she claps her wings,
The morn not waking till she sings.
Hark, hark, with what a pretty throat,
Poor robin redbreast tunes his note;
Hark how the jolly cuckoos sing,
Cuckoo to welcome in the spring!
Cuckoo to welcome in the spring!

[1] "Harmony written or pricked down in opposition to plain-song, where the descant rested with the will of the singer."—*Chappell.* (The nightingale's song, being full of rich variety, is often termed *prick-song* by old writers. So they speak of the cuckoo's *plain-song.*)

[2] "Hark, hark! the lark at heaven's gate sings."
Cymbeline, iii. 2.

From JOHN LYLY'S *Sappho and Phao*, 1584.

O CRUEL LOVE!

O CRUEL Love, on thee I lay
My curse, which shall strike blind the day;
Never may sleep with velvet hand
Charm thine eyes with sacred wand;
Thy jailors shall be hopes and fears,
Thy prison-mates groans, sighs, and tears,
Thy play to wear out weary times,
Fantastic passions, vows, and rhymes;
Thy bread be frowns, thy drink be gall,
Such as when you Phao call;
The bed thou liest on be[1] despair,
Thy sleep fond dreams, thy dreams long care.
Hope, like thy fool at thy bed's head,
Mock[2] thee till madness strike thee dead,
As, Phao, thou dost me with thy proud eyes;
In thee poor Sappho lives, for thee she dies.

[1] Old ed. "by." [2] Old ed. "mockes."

JOHN LYLY.

VULCAN'S SONG.

MY shag-hair Cyclops, come, let's ply
  Our Lemnian hammers lustily.
    By my wife's sparrows,
    I swear these arrows
    Shall singing fly
    Through many a wanton's eye.

These headed are with golden blisses,
These silver ones feathered with kisses;
    But this of lead
    Strikes a clown dead,
    When in a dance
    He falls in a trance,
To see his black-brow lass not buss him,
And then whines out for death t' untruss him.
So, so: our work being done, let's play:
Holiday, boys! cry holiday!

From JOHN LYLY'S *Endymion*,
1591.

PAGES AND THE WATCH.

Watch. STAND! who goes there?
We charge you appear
'Fore our constable here,
In the name of the Man in the Moon.
To us billmen relate,
Why you stagger so late,
And how you come drunk so soon.
Pages. What are ye, scabs?
Watch. The watch :
This the constable.
Pages. A patch !
Constable. Knock 'em down unless they all stand ;
If any run away,
'Tis the old watchman's play,
To reach him a bill of his hand.
Pages. O gentlemen, hold,
Your gowns freeze with cold,
And your rotten teeth dance in your head.
Wine nothing shall cost ye ;
Nor huge fires to roast ye;
Then soberly let us be led.
Constable. Come, my brown bills, we'll roar,
Bounce loud at tavern door.
Omnes. And i' th' morning steal all to bed.

FAIRY REVELS.

Omnes. PINCH him, pinch him, black and blue,
　　　　　Saucy mortals must not view
　　　　What the queen of stars is doing,
　　　　Nor pry into our fairy wooing.
1 *Fairy.*　　Pinch him blue—
2 *Fairy.*　　And pinch him black—
3 *Fairy.*　　Let him not lack
　　　　Sharp nails to pinch him blue and red,
　　　　Till sleep has rocked his addlehead.
4 *Fairy.* For the trespass he hath done,
　　　　Spots o'er all his flesh shall run.
　　　　Kiss Endymion, kiss his eyes,
　　　　Then to our midnight heidegyes.[1]

[1] Rustic dances.

From JOHN LYLY'S *Galathea*, 1592.

CUPID ARRAIGNED.

O YES, O yes! if any maid
Whom leering Cupid has betrayed
To frowns of spite, to eyes of scorn,
And would in madness now see torn
The boy in pieces, let her come
Hither, and lay on him her doom.

O yes, O yes! has any lost
A heart which many a sigh hath cost?
Is any cozened of a tear
Which as a pearl disdain does wear?
Here stands the thief; let her but come
Hither, and lay on him her doom.

Is any one undone by fire,
And turned to ashes through desire?
Did ever any lady weep,
Being cheated of her golden sleep
Stolen by sick thoughts?—the pirate's found,
And in her tears he shall be drowned.

Read his indictment, let him hear
What he's to trust to. Boy, give ear!

JOHN LYLY.

From JOHN LYLY'S *Midas*, 1592.

DAPHNE.

My Daphne's hair is twisted gold,
   Bright stars a-piece her eyes do hold,
My Daphne's brow enthrones the graces,
My Daphne's beauty stains all faces;
On Daphne's cheek grow rose and cherry,
On Daphne's lip a sweeter berry;
Daphne's snowy hand but touched does melt,
And then no heavenlier warmth is felt;
My Daphne's voice tunes all the spheres,
My Daphne's music charms all ears;
Fond am I thus to sing her praise,
These glories now are turned to bays.

SYRINX.

PAN'S Syrinx was a girl indeed,
  Though now she's turned into a reed ;
From that dear reed Pan's pipe does come,
A pipe that strikes Apollo dumb ;
Nor flute, nor lute, nor gittern can
So chant it as the pipe of Pan :
Cross-gartered swains and dairy girls,
With faces smug and round as pearls,
When Pan's shrill pipe begins to play,
With dancing wear out night and day ;
The bagpipe's drone his hum lays by,
When Pan sounds up his minstrelsy ;
His minstrelsy ! O base ! this quill,
Which at my mouth with wind I fill,
Puts me in mind, though her I miss,
That still my Syrinx' lips I kiss.

SONG TO APOLLO.

SING to Apollo, god of day,
Whose golden beams with morning play,
And make her eyes so brightly shine,
Aurora's face is called divine ;
Sing to Phœbus and that throne
Of diamonds which he sits upon.
    Io, pæans let us sing
    To Physic's and to Poesy's king !

Crown all his altars with bright fire,
Laurels bind about his lyre,
A Daphnean coronet for his head,
The Muses dance about his bed ;
When on his ravishing lute he plays,
Strew his temple round with bays.
    Io, pæans let us sing
    To the glittering Delian king !

From JOHN LYLY'S *Mother Bombie*, 1594.

IO, BACCHUS!

Omnes.   IO, Bacchus! To thy table
      Thou call'st every drunken rabble;
      We already are stiff drinkers,
      Then seal us for thy jolly skinkers.[1]
1.   Wine, O wine,
     O juice divine,
     How dost thou the nowle[2] refine!
2. Plump thou mak'st men's ruby faces,
   And from girls canst fetch embraces.
3. By thee our noses swell
   With sparkling carbuncle.
4. O the dear blood of grapes
   Turns us to antic shapes,
   Now to show tricks like apes,
1. Now lion-like to roar,
2. Now goatishly to whore,
3. Now hoggishly i' th' mire,
4. Now flinging hats i' th' fire.

Omnes. Io, Bacchus! at thy table,
     Make us of thy reeling rabble.

---

[1] Drawers, tapsters.   [2] Head, wits.

LOVE'S COLLEGE.

O CUPID! monarch over kings,
Wherefore hast thou feet and wings?
It is to show how swift thou art,
When thou woundest a tender heart!
Thy wings being clipped, and feet held still,
Thy bow so many could not kill.

It is all one in Venus' wanton school,
Who highest sits, the wise man or the fool.
   Fools in love's college
   Have far more knowledge
   To read a woman over,
   Than a neat prating lover:
     Nay, 'tis confessed,
     That fools please women best.

From GEORGE PEELE'S *The Arraignment of Paris*, 1584.

FAIR AND FAIR, AND TWICE SO FAIR.

Œnone. FAIR and fair, and twice so fair,
  As fair as any may be ;
 The fairest shepherd on our green,
  A love for any lady.
Paris. Fair and fair and twice so fair,
  As fair as any may be ;
 Thy love is fair for thee alone,
  And for no other lady.
Œn. My love is fair, my love is gay,
  As fresh as bin the flowers in May,
 And of my love my roundelay,
 My merry, merry, merry roundelay,
 Concludes with Cupid's curse,—
  They that do change old love for new,
  Pray gods they change for worse !
Ambo simul. They that do change, &c.
 Œn. Fair and fair, &c.
 Par. Fair and fair, &c.
  Thy love is fair, &c.
Œn. My love can pipe, my love can sing,
 My love can many a pretty thing,
 And of his lovely praises ring
 My merry, merry roundelays,
  Amen to Cupid's curse,
 They that do change, &c.
Par. They that do change, &c.
Ambo. Fair and fair, &c.

THE SAD SHEPHERD'S PASSION OF LOVE.

O GENTLE Love, ungentle for thy deed,
    Thou makest my heart
    A bloody mark
With piercing shot to bleed.
Shoot soft, sweet Love, for fear thou shoot amiss,
    For fear too keen
    Thy arrows been,
And hit the heart where my beloved is.
Too fair that fortune were, nor never I
    Shall be so blest,
    Among the rest,
That Love shall seize on her by sympathy.
Then since with Love my prayers bear no boot,
    This doth remain
    To cease my pain,
I take the wound, and die at Venus' foot.

ŒNONE'S COMPLAINT.

MELPOMENE, the muse of tragic songs,
With mournful tunes, in stole of dismal hue,
Assist a silly nymph to wail her woe,
And leave thy lusty company behind.

Thou luckless wreath! becomes not me to wear
The poplar tree for triumph of my love :
Then as my joy, my pride of love, is left,
Be thou unclothed of thy lovely green ;

And in thy leaves my fortune written be,
And them some gentle wind let blow abroad,
That all the world may see how false of love
False Paris hath to his Œnone been.

THE SHEPHERDS' DIRGE FOR POOR COLIN.

WELLADAY, welladay, poor Colin, thou art going
  to the ground,
 The love whom Thestylis hath slain,
 Hard heart, fair face, fraught with disdain,
Disdain in love a deadly wound.
 Wound her, sweet Love, so deep again,
 That she may feel the dying pain
 Of this unhappy shepherd's swain,
And die for love as Colin died, as Colin died.

From GEORGE PEELE'S *Polyhymnia*, 1590.

FAREWELL TO ARMS.

HIS golden locks time hath to silver turned;
    O time too swift, O swiftness never ceasing!
His youth 'gainst time and age hath ever spurned,
    But spurned in vain; youth waneth by increasing:
Beauty, strength, youth, are flowers but fading seen;
Duty, faith, love, are roots, and ever green.

His helmet now shall make a hive for bees,
    And, lovers' sonnets turned to holy psalms,
A man-at-arms must now serve on his knees,
    And feed on prayers, which are age his alms:
But though from court to cottage he depart,
His saint is sure of his unspotted heart.

And when he saddest sits in homely cell,
    He'll teach his swains this carol for a song,—
" Blessed be the hearts that wish my sovereign well,
    Cursed be the souls that think her any wrong."
Goddess, allow this aged man his right,
To be your beadsman now that was your knight.

From GEORGE PEELE'S *The Hunting of Cupid*, licensed for publication in 1591.

CORIDON AND MELAMPUS' SONG.

Cor. MELAMPUS, when will love be void of fears?
Mel. When jealousy hath neither eyes nor ears.
Cor. Melampus, when will love be thoroughly shrieved?
Mel. When it is hard to speak, and not believed.
Cor. Melampus, when is love most malcontent?
Mel. When lovers range and bear their bows unbent.
Cor. Melampus, tell me when love takes least harm?
Mel. When swains' sweet pipes are puffed, and trulls are warm.
Cor. Melampus, tell me when is love best fed?
Mel. When it has sucked the sweet that ease hath bred.
Cor. Melampus, when is time in love ill-spent?
Mel. When it earns meed and yet receives no rent.
Cor. Melampus, when is time well-spent in love?
Mel. When deeds win meed, and words love-works do prove.

CUPID'S ARROWS.

AT Venus' entreaty for Cupid her son
These arrows by Vulcan were cunningly done.
The first is Love, as here you may behold,
His feathers, head, and body, are of gold:
The second shaft is Hate, a foe to love,
And bitter are his torments for to prove:
The third is Hope, from whence our comfort springs,
His feathers [they] are pulled from Fortune's wings:
Fourth Jealousy in basest minds doth dwell;
His metal Vulcan's Cyclops sent from hell.

WHAT THING IS LOVE?

WHAT thing is love? for, well I wot, love is a thing.
It is a prick, it is a sting,
It is a pretty, pretty thing;
It is a fire, it is a coal,
Whose flame creeps in at every hole;
And as my wit doth best devise,
Love's dwelling is in ladies' eyes:
From whence do glance love's piercing darts
That make such holes into our hearts;
And all the world herein accord
Love is a great and mighty lord,
And when he list to mount so high,
With Venus he in heaven doth lie,
And evermore hath been a god
Since Mars and she played even and odd.

From GEORGE PEELE'S *The Old Wives' Tale*, 1595.

THE IMPATIENT MAID.

WHENAS the rye reach to the chin,
And chopcherry, chopcherry ripe within,
Strawberries swimming in the cream,
And schoolboys playing in the stream;
Then, O, then, O, then, O, my true love said,
'Till that time come again
She could not live a maid.

HARVESTMEN A-SINGING.

ALL ye that lovely lovers be,
Pray you for me:
Lo, here we come a-sowing, a-sowing,
And sow sweet fruits of love;
In your sweet hearts well may it prove!

Lo, here we come a-reaping, a-reaping,
To reap our harvest-fruit!
And thus we pass the year so long,
And never be we mute.

SPREAD, TABLE, SPREAD.

SPREAD, table, spread,
Meat, drink, and bread,
Ever may I have
What I ever crave,
When I am spread,
Meat for my black cock,
And meat for my red.

CELANTA AT THE WELL OF LIFE.

A Head comes up with ears of corn, and she combs them in her lap.

Voice.

GENTLY dip, but not too deep,
For fear you make the golden beard to weep.
Fair maiden, white and red,
Comb me smooth, and stroke my head,
And thou shalt have some cockell-bread.

A Second Head comes up full of gold, which she combs into her lap.

Sec. Head. Gently dip, but not too deep,
For fear thou make the golden beard to weep.
Fair maid, white and red,
Comb me smooth, and stroke my head,
And every hair a sheaf shall be,
And every sheaf a golden tree.

From GEORGE PEELE'S *David and Bethsabe,* 1599.

BETHSABE BATHING.

HOT sun, cool fire, tempered with sweet air,
Black shade, fair nurse, shadow my white hair:
Shine, sun; burn, fire; breathe, air, and ease me;
Black shade, fair nurse, shroud me, and please me:
Shadow, my sweet nurse, keep me from burning,
Make not my glad cause cause of mourning.
    Let not my beauty's fire
    Inflame unstaid desire,
    Nor pierce any bright eye
    That wandereth lightly.

From LODGE and GREENE's *A Looking Glass for London and England*, 1594.

DO ME RIGHT AND DO ME REASON.

BEAUTY, alas ! where wast thou born,
Thus to hold thyself in scorn ?
Whenas Beauty kissed to woo thee,
Thou by Beauty dost undo me :
 Heigh-ho ! despise me not.

I and thou in sooth are one,
Fairer thou, I fairer none :
Wanton thou, and wilt thou, wanton,
Yield a cruel heart to plant on ?
Do me right, and do me reason ;
Cruelty is cursed treason :
  Heigh-ho ! I love, heigh-ho ! I love,
  Heigh-ho ! and yet he eyes me not.

From THOMAS NASHE'S *Summer's
Last Will and Testament,*
1600.

SPRING, THE SWEET SPRING.

SPRING, the sweet Spring, is the year's pleasant king;
Then blooms each thing, then maids dance in a ring,
Cold doth not sting, the pretty birds do sing,
Cuckoo, jug, jug, pu we, to witta woo.

The palm and may make country houses gay,
Lambs frisk and play, the shepherds pipe all day,
And we hear aye birds tune this merry lay,
Cuckoo, jug, jug, pu we, to witta woo.

The fields breathe sweet, the daisies kiss our feet,
Young lovers meet, old wives a-sunning sit,
In every street these tunes our ears do greet,
Cuckoo, jug, jug, pu we, to witta woo.
    Spring, the sweet spring!

A-MAYING, A-PLAYING.

TRIP and go ! heave and ho !
Up and down, to and fro,
From the town to the grove,
Two and two, let us rove
A-maying, a-playing :
Love hath no gainsaying,
So merrily trip and go !

FADING SUMMER.

FAIR summer droops, droop men and beasts therefore,
So fair a summer look for never more :
All good things vanish less than in a day,
Peace, plenty, pleasure, suddenly decay.
   Go not yet away, bright soul of the sad year,
   The earth is hell when thou leav'st to appear.
What, shall those flowers that decked thy garland erst,
Upon thy grave be wastefully dispersed ?
O trees, consume your sap in sorrow's source,
Streams, turn to tears your tributary course.
   Go not yet hence, bright soul of the sad year,
   The earth is hell when thou leav'st to appear.

WINTER, PLAGUE, AND PESTILENCE.

AUTUMN hath all the summer's fruitful treasure ;
Gone is our sport, fled is our Croydon's pleasure !
Short days, sharp days, long nights come on apace :
Ah, who shall hide us from the winter's face ?
Cold doth increase, the sickness will not cease,
And here we lie, God knows, with little ease.
    From winter, plague and pestilence, good Lord,
        deliver us !

London doth mourn, Lambeth is quite forlorn !
Trades cry, woe worth that ever they were born !
The want of term is town and city's harm ;
Close chambers we do want to keep us warm.
Long banished must we live from our friends :
This low-built house will bring us to our ends.
    From winter, plague and pestilence, good Lord,
        deliver us !

DEATH'S SUMMONS.

ADIEU ; farewell earth's bliss,
This world uncertain is :
Fond are life's lustful joys,
Death proves them all but toys.
None from his darts can fly :
I am sick, I must die.
           Lord have mercy on us !

Rich men, trust not in wealth,
Gold cannot buy you health ;
Physic himself must fade ;
All things to end are made ;
The plague full swift goes by ;
I am sick, I must die.
           Lord have mercy on us !

Beauty is but a flower,
Which wrinkles will devour :
Brightness falls from the air ;
Queens have died young and fair ;
Dust hath closed Helen's eye ;
I am sick, I must die.
           Lord have mercy on us !

Strength stoops unto the grave :
Worms feed on Hector brave ;
Swords may not fight with fate :
Earth still holds ope her gate.
Come, come, the bells do cry ;
I am sick, I must die.
           Lord have mercy on us !

Wit with his wantonness,
Tasteth death's bitterness.
Hell's executioner
Hath no ears for to hear
What vain art can reply ;
I am sick, I must die.
           Lord have mercy on us !

Haste therefore each degree
To welcome destiny :
Heaven is our heritage,
Earth but a player's stage.
Mount we unto the sky ;
I am sick, I must die.
           Lord have mercy on us !

From *The Two Gentlemen of Verona*.

SILVIA.

WHO is Silvia? what is she,
  That all our swains commend her?
Holy, fair, and wise is she;
  The heaven such grace did lend her,
That she might admired be.

Is she kind as she is fair?
  For beauty lives with kindness.
Love doth to her eyes repair,
  To help him of his blindness;
And, being helped, inhabits there.

Then to Silvia let us sing,
  That Silvia is excelling;
She excels each mortal thing,
  Upon the dull earth dwelling:
To her let us garlands bring.

From *Love's Labour's Lost*.

THE RHYME OF WHITE AND RED.

IF she be made of white and red,
  Her faults will ne'er be known,
For blushing cheeks by faults are bred,
  And fears by pale white shown:
Then if she fear, or be to blame,
  By this you shall not know,
For still her cheeks possess the same,
  Which native she doth owe.[1]

[1] An old form of "own."

BIRON'S CANZONET.

IF love make me forsworn, how shall I swear to love?
   Ah, never faith could hold, if not to beauty vowed!
Though to myself forsworn, to thee I'll faithful prove;
   Those thoughts to me were oaks, to thee like osiers bowed.
Study his bias leaves, and makes his book thine eyes,
   Where all those pleasures live that art would comprehend;
If knowledge be the mark, to know thee shall suffice;
   Well learned is that tongue that well can thee commend,
All ignorant that soul that sees thee without wonder;
   (Which is to me some praise, that I thy parts admire;)
Thy eye Jove's lightning bears, thy voice his dreadful thunder,
   Which, not to anger bent, is music, and sweet fire.
Celestial as thou art, oh, pardon love this wrong,
That sings heaven's praise with such an earthly tongue!

THE LOVER'S TEARS.

SO sweet a kiss the golden sun gives not
To those fresh morning drops upon the rose,
As thy eye-beams, when their fresh rays have smote
The night of dew that on my cheeks down flows:
Nor shines the silver moon one half so bright
Through the transparent bosom of the deep,
As doth thy face through tears of mine give light:
Thou shinest in every tear that I do weep;
No drop but as a coach doth carry thee,
So ridest thou triumphing in my woe:
Do but behold the tears that swell in me,
And they thy glory through my grief will show:
But do not love thyself; then thou wilt keep
My tears for glasses, and still make me weep.
O queen of queens, how far dost thou excel!
No thought can think, nor tongue of mortal tell.

PERJURY EXCUSED.

DID not the heavenly rhetoric of thine eye,
   'Gainst whom the world cannot hold argument,
Persuade my heart to this false perjury?
   Vows for thee broke deserve not punishment.
A woman I forswore; but I will prove,
   Thou being a goddess, I forswore not thee:
My vow was earthly, thou a heavenly love;
   Thy grace being gained cures all disgrace in me.
Vows are but breath, and breath a vapour is:
   Then thou, fair sun, which on my earth dost shine,
Exhalest this vapour-vow; in thee it is:
   If broken then, it is no fault of mine:
If by me broke, what fool is not so wise
To lose an oath to win a paradise?

ON A DAY—ALACK THE DAY!

ON a day—alack the day!—
　Love, whose month is ever May,
Spied a blossom, passing fair,
Playing in the wanton air:
Through the velvet leaves the wind,
All unseen, 'gan passage find;
That the lover, sick to death,
Wish himself the heaven's breath.
Air, quoth he, thy cheeks may blow;
Air, would I might triumph so!
But, alack, my hand is sworn,
Ne'er to pluck thee from thy thorn:
Vow, alack, for youth unmeet,
Youth so apt to pluck a sweet.
Do not call it sin in me,
That I am forsworn for thee:
Thou for whom Jove would swear
Juno but an Ethiope were;
And deny himself for Jove,
Turning mortal for thy love.

SPRING AND WINTER.

WHEN daisies pied, and violets blue,
　　And lady-smocks all silver-white,
And cuckoo-buds of yellow hue,
　Do paint the meadows with delight,
The cuckoo then, on every tree,
Mocks married men, for thus sings he,
　　　　Cuckoo;
Cuckoo, cuckoo,—O word of fear,
Unpleasing to a married ear!

When shepherds pipe on oaten straws,
   And merry larks are ploughmen's clocks,
When turtles tread, and rooks, and daws,
   And maidens bleach their summer smocks,
The cuckoo then, on every tree,
Mocks married men, for thus sings he,.
      Cuckoo;
Cuckoo, cuckoo,—O word of fear,
Unpleasing to a married ear!

When icicles hang by the wall,
   And Dick the shepherd blows his nail,
And Tom bears logs into the hall,
   And milk comes frozen home in pail,
When blood is nipped, and ways be-foul,
Then nightly sings the staring owl,
      To-whit;
      To-who, a merry note,
While greasy Joan doth keel[1] the pot.

When all around the wind doth blow,
   And coughing drowns the parson's saw,
And birds sit brooding in the snow,
   And Marian's nose looks red and raw,
When roasted crabs hiss in the bowl,
Then nightly sings the staring owl,
      To-whit;
      To-who, a merry note,
While greasy Joan doth keel the pot.

[1] Skim.

From *A Midsummer Night's Dream.*

OVER HILL, OVER DALE.

OVER hill, over dale,
   Thorough bush, thorough brier,
Over park, over pale,
   Thorough flood, thorough fire,
I do wander everywhere,
Swifter than the moon's sphere ;
And I serve the fairy queen,
To dew her orbs upon the green.
The cowslips tall her pensioners be ;
In their gold coats spots you see,
Those be rubies, fairy favours,
In those freckles live their savours :
I must go seek some dewdrops here,
And hang a pearl in every cowslip's ear.

YOU SPOTTED SNAKES WITH DOUBLE TONGUE.

YOU spotted snakes with double tongue,
    Thorny hedge-hogs, be not seen;
Newts, and blind-worms, do no wrong;
    Come not near our fairy queen:
    Philomel, with melody,
    Sing in our sweet lullaby;
Lulla, lulla, lullaby, lulla, lulla, lullaby;
    Never harm,
    Nor spell, nor charm,
    Come our lovely lady nigh;
    So, good night, with lullaby.
Weaving spiders, come not here:
    Hence, you long-legged spinners, hence!
Beetles black, approach not near;
    Worm, nor snail, do no offence.
    Philomel, with melody, &c.

THE OUSEL-COCK, SO BLACK OF HUE.

THE ousel-cock, so black of hue,
    With orange-tawny bill,
The throstle with his note so true,
    The wren with little quill;
The finch, the sparrow, and the lark,
    The plain-song [1] cuckoo gray,
Whose note full many a man doth mark,
    And dares not answer nay.

[1] See note 1, p. 2.

NOW THE HUNGRY LION ROARS.

NOW the hungry lion roars,
  And the wolf behowls the moon ;
Whilst the heavy ploughman snores,
  All with weary task fordone.
Now the wasted brands do glow,
  Whilst the scritch-owl, scritching loud,
Puts the wretch that lies in woe
  In remembrance of a shroud.
Now it is the time of night
  That the graves, all gaping wide,
Everyone lets forth his sprite,
  In the churchway paths to glide :
And we fairies, that do run
  By the triple Hecate's team,
From the presence of the sun,
  Following darkness like a dream,
Now are frolic ; not a mouse.
Shall disturb this hallowed house :
I am sent with broom before,
To sweep the dust behind the door.

Through the house give glimmering light,
  By the dead and drowsy fire ;
Every elf and fairy sprite
  Hop as light as bird from brier ;
And this ditty, after me, .
Sing, and dance it, trippingly.

First, rehearse your song by rote,
To each word a warbling note :
Hand in hand, with fairy grace,
Will we sing, and bless this place.

Now, until the break of day,
Through this house each fairy stray.
To the best bride-bed will we,
Which by us shall blessed be ;
And the issue there create
Ever shall be fortunate.
So shall all the couples three
Ever true in loving be ;
And the blots of Nature's hand
Shall not in their issue stand ;
Never mole, hare-lip, nor scar,
Nor mark prodigious, such as are
Despised in nativity,
Shall upon their children be.
With this field-dew consecrate,
Every fairy take his gait ;
And each several chamber bless,
Through this palace with sweet peace :
And the owner of it blest,
Ever shall in safety rest.
 Trip away ;
 Make no stay :
Meet me all by break of day.

From *The Merchant of Venice.*

TELL ME WHERE IS FANCY BRED.

TELL me where is fancy bred,
  Or in the heart, or in the head?
How begot, how nourished?
    Reply, reply.

It is engendered in the eyes,
With gazing fed; and fancy dies
In the cradle where it lies:
Let us all ring fancy's knell;
I'll begin it,—Ding, dong, bell.
    Ding, dong, bell.

THE CASKETS.

Gold.

ALL that glisters is not gold,
  Often have you heard that told;
Many a man his life hath sold
But my outside to behold;
Gilded tombs do worms infold.
Had you been as wise as bold,
Young in limbs, in judgment old,
Your answer had not been inscrolled:
Fare you well; your suit is cold.

Silver.

The fire seven times tried this;
Seven times tried that judgment is
That did never choose amiss:
Some there be that shadows kiss;
Such have but a shadow's bliss.;
There be fools alive, I wis,
Silvered o'er; and so was this.
Take what wife you will to bed,
I will ever be your head:
So be gone: you are sped.

Lead.

You that choose not by the view,
Chance as fair, and choose as true!
Since this fortune falls to you,
Be content, and seek no new.
If you be well pleased with this,
And hold your fortune for your bliss,
Turn you where your lady is,
And claim her with a loving kiss.

From *Much Ado about Nothing.*

SIGH NO MORE, LADIES.

SIGH no more, ladies, sigh no more;
  Men were deceivers ever;
One foot in sea, and one on shore,
  To one thing constant never:
Then sigh not so, but let them go,
  And be you blithe and bonny,
Converting all your sounds of woe
  Into Hey nonny, nonny.

Sing no more ditties, sing no mo,
  Of dumps so dull and heavy;
The fraud of men was ever so,
  Since summer first was leavy:
    Then sigh not so, &c.

HERO'S EPITAPH.

DONE to death by slanderous tongues
  Was the Hero that here lies;
Death, in guerdon of her wrongs,
  Gives her fame which never dies:
So the life that died with shame,
Lives in death with glorious fame.

SONG OF WOE.

PARDON, goddess of the night,
    Those that slew thy virgin knight;
For the which, with songs of woe,
Round about her tomb they go.
  Midnight, assist our moan;
    Help us to sigh and groan,
      Heavily, heavily:
Graves, yawn and yield your dead,
Till death be uttered,
      Heavily, heavily.

From *The Merry Wives of Windsor.*

PINCH HIM, FAIRIES.

FY on sinful fantasy!
    Fy on lust and luxury!
Lust is but a bloody fire,
Kindled with unchaste desire,
Fed in heart; whose flames aspire,
As thoughts do blow them, higher and higher.
  Pinch him, fairies, mutually;
  Pinch him for his villainy;
Pinch him, and burn him, and turn him about,
Till candles, and star-light, and moon-shine be out.

From *Twelfth Night*.

O MISTRESS MINE, WHERE ARE YOU ROAMING?

O MISTRESS mine, where are you roaming?
  O, stay and hear; your true love's coming,
That can sing both high and low:
Trip no further, pretty sweeting;
Journeys end in lovers meeting,
  Every wise man's son doth know.

What is love? 'tis not hereafter;
Present mirth hath present laughter;
  What's to come is still unsure:
In delay there lies no plenty;
Then come kiss me, sweet-and-twenty,[1]
  Youth's a stuff will not endure.

SLAIN BY A FAIR CRUEL MAID.

COME away, come away, death,
  And in sad cypress let me be laid;
Fly away, fly away, breath;
I am slain by a fair cruel maid.
My shroud of white, stuck all with yew,
    O, prepare it!
My part of death, no one so true
    Did share it.

[1] "Sweet-and-twenty"—twenty times sweet. (A term of endearment.)

Not a flower, not a flower sweet,
On my black coffin let there be strown;
Not a friend, not a friend greet
My poor corpse, where my bones shall be thrown:
A thousand thousand sighs to save,
    Lay me, O, where
Sad true lover never find my grave,
    To weep there!

WHEN THAT I WAS AND A LITTLE TINY BOY.

WHEN that I was and a little tiny boy,
  With hey, ho, the wind and the rain,
A foolish thing was but a toy,
  For the rain it raineth every day.

But when I came to man's estate,
  With hey, ho, the wind and the rain,
'Gainst knaves and thieves men shut their gate,
  For the rain it raineth every day.

But when I came, alas! to wive,
  With hey, ho, the wind and the rain,
By swaggering could I never thrive,
  For the rain it raineth every day.

But when I came unto my beds,
  With hey, ho, the wind and the rain,
With toss-pots still had drunken heads,
  For the rain it raineth every day.

A great while ago the world begun,
  With hey, ho, the wind and the rain,
But that's all one, our play is done,
  And we'll strive to please you every day.

From *As You Like It.*

UNDER THE GREENWOOD-TREE.

UNDER the greenwood tree,
 Who loves to lie with me,
And turn his merry note
 Unto the sweet bird's throat,
Come hither, come hither, come hither;
 Here shall he see
  No enemy
But winter and rough weather.

Who doth ambition shun,
 And loves to live i' the sun,
Seeking the food he eats,
 And pleased with what he gets,
Come hither, come hither, come hither:
 Here shall he see
  No enemy.
But winter and rough weather.

If it do come to pass,
 That any man turn ass,
Leaving his wealth and ease,
 A stubborn will to please,
Ducdame,¹ ducdame, ducdame;
 Here shall he see,
  Gross fools as he,
An if he will come to me.

¹ A word of doubtful meaning.

MAN'S INGRATITUDE.

B LOW, blow, thou winter wind,
   Thou art not so unkind
  As man's ingratitude ;
 Thy tooth is not so keen,
 Because thou art not seen,.
  Although thy breath be rude.
Heigh ho ! sing, heigh ho ! unto the green holly :
Most friendship is feigning, most loving mere folly :
  Then, heigh ho, the holly !
  This life is most jolly.

  Freeze, freeze, thou bitter sky,.
  That dost not bite so nigh.
    As benefits forgot :
  Though thou the waters warp,
  Thy sting is not so sharp,
    As friend remembered not.
Heigh ho ! sing heigh ho ! &c.

ROSALIND.

F ROM the east to western Ind,
   No jewel is like Rosalind.
Her worth, being mounted on the wind,
Through all the world bears Rosalind.
All the pictures, fairest lined,
Are but black to Rosalind.
Let no fair be kept in mind,
But the fair of Rosalind.

BEAUTY'S EPITOME.

WHY should this a desert be?
    For it is unpeopled? No;
Tongues I'll hang on every tree,
    That shall civil sayings show.
Some, how brief the life of man
    Runs his erring pilgrimage;
That the stretching of a span
    Buckles in his sum of age.
Some, of violated vows
    'Twixt the souls of friend and friend:
But upon the fairest boughs,
    Or at every sentence' end,
Will I Rosalinda write,
    Teaching all that read to know
The quintessence of every sprite
    Heaven would in little show.
Therefore heaven nature charged
    That one body should be filled
With all graces wide-enlarged:
    Nature presently distilled
Helen's cheek, but not her heart,
    Cleopatra's majesty,
Atalanta's better part,
    Sad Lucretia's modesty.
Thus Rosalind of many parts
    By heavenly synod was devised;
Of many faces, eyes, and hearts,
    To have the touches dearest prized.
Heaven would that she these gifts should have,
And I to live and die her slave.

WILLIAM SHAKESPEARE.

THE LOVE-LETTER.

ART thou god to shepherd turned,
That a maiden's heart hath burned?
Why, thy godhead laid apart,
Warr'st thou with a woman's heart?
Whiles the eye of man did woo me,
That could do no vengeance to me.
If the scorn of your bright eyne
Have power to raise such love in mine,
Alack, in me what strange effect
Would they work in mild aspect?
Whiles you chid me, I did love;
How then might your prayers move?
He that brings this love to thee,
Little knows this love in me:
And by him seal up thy mind;
Whether that thy youth and kind
Will the faithful offer take
Of me, and all that I can make;
Or else by him my love deny,
And then I'll study how to die.

IT WAS A LOVER AND HIS LASS.

IT was a lover and his lass,
  With a hey, and a ho, and a hey nonino,
That o'er the green corn-field did pass
  In the spring time, the only pretty ring time,
When birds do sing, hey ding a ding, ding;
Sweet lovers love the spring.

Between the acres of the rye,
  With a hey, and a ho, and a hey nonino,
These pretty country folks would lie,
  In spring time, &c.

This carol they began that hour,
  With a hey, and a ho, and a hey nonino,
How that a life was but a flower
  In spring time, &c.

And therefore take the present time,
  With a hey, and a ho, and a hey nonino,
For love is crowned with the prime,
  In spring time, &c.

TO LOVE AND WED FOR LOVE IS PERFECT BLISS.

THEN is there mirth in heaven,
  When earthly things made even
    Atone together.
Good duke, receive thy daughter:
Hymen from heaven brought her,
    Yea, brought her hither,
That thou might'st join her hand with his
Whose heart within his bosom is.

A WEDLOCK-HYMN.

WEDDING is great Juno's crown;
  O blessed bond of board and bed!
'Tis Hymen peoples every town;
  High wedlock then be honoured:
Honour, high honour and renown,
To Hymen, god of every town!

From Measure for Measure.

TAKE, O, TAKE THOSE LIPS AWAY.

TAKE, O, take those lips away,
  That so sweetly were forsworn;
And those eyes, the break of day,
  Lights that do mislead the morn:
But my kisses bring again,
        Bring again;
Seals of love but sealed in vain,
        Sealed in vain.

WILLIAM SHAKESPEARE.

From *Hamlet*.

HOW SHOULD I YOUR TRUE LOVE KNOW?

HOW should I your true love know
  From another one?
By his cockle hat and staff,
  And his sandal shoon.

He is dead and gone, lady,
  He is dead and gone;
At his head a grass-green turf,
  At his heels a stone.

White his shroud as the mountain snow,
  Larded all with sweet flowers,
Which bewept to the grave did go
  With true-love showers.

AND WILL HE NOT COME AGAIN?

AND will he not come again?
  And will he not come again?
  No, no, he is dead:
  Go to thy death-bed:
He never will come again.

His beard was as white as snow,
All flaxen was his poll:
  He is gone, he is gone,
  And we cast away moan;
God ha' mercy on his soul!

From *Macbeth*.

THE WITCHES' CAULDRON.

1 *Witch.* THRICE the brinded cat hath mewed.
2 *Witch.* Thrice and once the hedge-pig whined.
3 *Witch.* Harpier cries 'Tis time, 'tis time.
1 *Witch.* Round about the cauldron go :
        In the poisoned entrails throw.
        Toad, that under cold stone
        Days and nights has thirty-one,
        Sweltered venom sleeping got,
        Boil thou first i' the charmed pot!
All. Double, double toil and trouble;
        Fire burn, and cauldron bubble.

2 *Witch.* Fillet of a fenny snake,
        In the cauldron boil and bake;
        Eye of newt and toe of frog,
        Wool of bat and tongue of dog,
        Adder's fork and blind-worm's sting,
        Lizard's leg and owlet's wing,
        For a charm of powerful trouble;
        Like a hell-broth boil and bubble.
All. Double, double toil and trouble ;
        Fire burn, and cauldron bubble.

3 *Witch.* Scale of dragon, tooth of wolf,
        Witches' mummy, maw, and gulf
        Of the ravined salt-sea shark,
        Root of hemlock digged i' the dark,

Liver of blaspheming Jew,
Gall of goat, and slips of yew,
Slivered in the moon's eclipse,
Nose of Turk and Tartar's lips,
Finger of birth-strangled babe
Ditch-delivered by a drab,
Make the gruel thick and slab;
Add thereto a tiger's chaudron,
For the ingredients of our cauldron.
All. Double, double toil and trouble;
Fire burn, and cauldron bubble.

2 *Witch.* Cool it with a baboon's blood,
Then the charm is firm and good.

From *Cymbeline.*

HARK! HARK! THE LARK AT HEAVEN'S GATE SINGS.

HARK! hark! the lark at heaven's gate sings,
 And Phœbus 'gins arise,
His steeds to water at those springs
 On chaliced flowers that lies;
And winking Mary-buds begin
 To ope their golden eyes;
With every thing that pretty is,
 My lady sweet, arise;
  Arise, arise.

FEAR NO MORE THE HEAT OF THE SUN.

FEAR no more the heat o' the sun
    Nor the furious winter's rages;
Thou thy worldly task hast done,
    Home art gone, and ta'en thy wages:
Golden lads and girls all must,
As chimney-sweepers, come to dust.

Fear no more the frown o' the great,
    Thou art past the tyrant's stroke;
Care no more to clothe, and eat;
    To thee the reed is as the oak:
The sceptre, learning, physic, must
All follow this, and come to dust.

Fear no more the lightning-flash,
    Nor the all-dreaded thunder-stone;
Fear not slander, censure rash;
    Thou hast finished joy and moan:
All lovers young, all lovers must
Consign to thee, and come to dust.

No exorciser harm thee!
Nor no witchcraft charm thee!
Ghost unlaid forbear thee!
Nothing ill come near thee!
Quiet consummation have;
And renowned be thy grave!

From *Antony and Cleopatra*.

COME, THOU MONARCH OF THE VINE.

COME, thou monarch of the vine,
Plumpy Bacchus with pink eyne!
In thy fats our cares be drowned,
With thy grapes our hairs be crowned:
  Cup us till the world go round,
  Cup us till the world go round!

From *A Winter's Tale*.

WHEN DAFFODILS BEGIN TO PEER.

WHEN daffodils begin to peer,
  With heigh! the doxy over the dale,
Why, then comes in the sweet o' the year;
  For the red blood reigns in the winter's pale.

The white sheet bleaching on the hedge,
  With heigh! the sweet birds, O, how they sing!
Doth set my pugging [1] tooth on edge;
  For a quart of ale is a dish for a king.

The lark, that tirra-lirra chants,
  With heigh! with heigh! the thrush and the jay:
Are summer songs for me and my aunts,
  While we lie tumbling in the hay.

[1] Thievish.

A MERRY HEART GOES ALL THE DAY.

JOG on, jog on, the footpath way,
    And merrily hent the stile-a:
A merry heart goes all the day,
    Your sad tires in a mile-a.

COME BUY, COME BUY.

LAWN as white as driven snow;
    Cypress black as e'er was crow;
Gloves as sweet as damask roses;
Masks for faces, and for noses;
Bugle-bracelet, necklace-amber,
Perfume for a lady's chamber:
Golden quoifs and stomachers,
For my lads to give their dears;
Pins and poking-sticks [1] of steel,
What maids lack from head to heel:
    Come buy of me, come; come buy, come buy;
    Buy, lads, or else your lasses cry:
    Come buy.

---

[1] Sticks of steel for setting the plaits of a ruff.

COME TO THE PEDLAR.

WILL you buy any tape,
　　Or lace for your cape,
My dainty duck, my dear-a?
　Any silk, any thread,
　Any toys for your head,
Of the new'st and finest, finest wear-a?
　Come to the pedlar;
　Money's a medler,
That doth utter all men's ware-a.

From *The Tempest*.

COME UNTO THESE YELLOW SANDS.

COME unto these yellow sands,
　　And then take hands:
Courtsied when you have and kissed
　The wild waves whist,
Foot it featly here and there;
And, sweet sprites, the burden bear.
　Hark, hark!
　　Bow-wow.
　The watch-dogs bark:
　　Bow-wow.
　Hark, hark! I hear
The strain of strutting chanticleer
Cry, Cock-a-didle-dow.

WILLIAM SHAKESPEARE.

A DIRGE.

FULL fathom five thy father lies:
  Of his bones are coral made;
Those are pearls that were his eyes:
  Nothing of him that doth fade
But doth suffer a sea-change
Into something rich and strange.
Sea-nymphs hourly ring his knell:
Hark! now I hear them,—ding-dong, bell.

SHAKE OFF SLUMBER, AND BEWARE.

WHILE you here do snoring lie,
  Open-eyed Conspiracy
  His time doth take;
If of life you keep a care,
Shake off slumber, and beware:
  Awake! awake!

WHERE THE BEE SUCKS, THERE SUCK I.

WHERE the bee sucks, there suck I;
  In a cowslip's bell I lie;
There I couch when owls do cry;
On the bat's back I do fly
After summer merrily:
Merrily, merrily, shall I live now
Under the blossom that hangs on the bough.

From BEN JONSON's *Cynthia's Revels*, 1601.

SLOW, SLOW, FRESH FOUNT.

SLOW, slow, fresh fount, keep time with my salt
    tears ;
  Yet slower, yet ; O faintly, gentle springs ;
List to the heavy part the music bears,
    Woe weeps out her division when she sings.
        Droop herbs and flowers ;
        Fall grief in showers,
        Our beauties are not ours ;
        O, I could still,
Like melting snow upon some craggy hill,
        Drop, drop, drop, drop,
Since nature's pride is now a withered daffodil.

THE KISS.

O THAT joy so soon should waste !
  Or so sweet a bliss
  As a kiss
Might not for ever last !
So sugared, so melting, so soft, so delicious,
  The dew that lies on roses,
  When the morn herself discloses,
Is not so precious.
O rather than I would it smother,
Were I to taste such another ;
  It should be my wishing
  That I might die kissing.

THE GLOVE.

THOU more than most sweet glove,
  Unto my more sweet love,
Suffer me to store with kisses
This empty lodging that now misses
  The pure rosy hand that ware thee,
  Whiter than the kid that bare thee.
    Thou art soft, but that was softer;
    Cupid's self hath kissed it ofter
    Than e'er he did his mother's doves,
    Supposing her the queen of loves,
    That was thy mistress, best of gloves.

HYMN TO DIANA.

QUEEN, and huntress, chaste and fair,
  Now the sun is laid to sleep,
Seated in thy silver chair,
  State in wonted manner keep:
    Hesperus entreats thy light,
    Goddess excellently bright.

Earth, let not thy envious shade
  Dare itself to interpose;
Cynthia's shining orb was made
  Heaven to clear when day did close:
    Bless us then with wished sight,
    Goddess excellently bright.

Lay thy bow of pearl apart,
  And thy crystal shining quiver;
Give unto the flying hart
  Space to breathe, how short soever:
    Thou that makest a day of night,
    Goddess excellently bright.

From BEN JONSON'S *The Poetaster*, 1601.

HIS SUPPOSED MISTRESS.

IF I freely may discover
What would please me in my lover,
I would have her fair and witty,
Savouring more of court than city ;
A little proud, but full of pity ;
Light and humorous in her toying ;
Oft building hopes, and soon destroying ;
Long, but sweet in the enjoying ;
Neither too easy nor too hard :
All extremes I would have barred.

She should be allowed her passions,
So they were but used as fashions ;
Sometimes froward, and then frowning,
Sometimes sickish, and then swowning,
Every fit with change still crowning.
Purely jealous I would have her,
Then only constant when I crave her ;
'Tis a virtue should not save her.
Thus, nor her delicates would cloy me,
Nor her peevishness annoy me.

LOVE IS BLIND, AND A WANTON.

LOVE is blind, and a wanton;
In the whole world, there is scant one
Such another:
No, not his mother.
He hath plucked her doves and sparrows,
To feather his sharp arrows,
And alone prevaileth,
While sick Venus waileth.
But if Cypris once recover
The wag, it shall behove her
To look better to him,
Or she will undo him.

ADDE MERUM!

WAKE, our mirth begins to die,
Quicken it with tunes and wine.
Raise your notes; you're out: fy, fy!
This drowsiness is an ill sign.
We banish him the quire of gods,
That droops again:
Then all are men,
For here's not one, but nods.

THE BANQUET OF SENSE.

1. THEN, in a free and lofty strain
    Our broken tunes we thus repair;
2. And we answer them again,
    Running division on the panting air;

Ambo. To celebrate this feast of sense,
    As free from scandal as offence.
1.   Here is beauty for the eye;
2.   For the ear sweet melody;
1. Ambrosiac odours for the smell;
2.   Delicious nectar for the taste;

Ambo. For the touch a lady's waist,
    Which doth all the rest excel.

From BEN JONSON'S *Volpone, or
The Fox*, 1607.

O FORTUNATI!

FOOLS, they are the only nation
    Worth men's envy or admiration;
Free from care or sorrow-taking,
Selves and others merry making:
All they speak or do is sterling.
Your fool he is your great man's dearling,
And your ladies' sport and pleasure;
Tongue and bable[1] are his treasure.
Ev'n his face begetteth laughter,
And he speaks truth free from slaughter;
He's the grace of every feast,
And sometimes the chiefest guest;
Hath his trencher and his stool,
When wit waits upon the fool.
    O, who would not be
      He, he, he?

[1] Old form of "bauble."

VIVAMUS, MEA LESBIA.

COME, my Celia, let us prove,
   While we can, the sports of love,
Time will not be ours for ever,
He, at length, our good will sever;
Spend not then his gifts in vain:
Suns that set may rise again;
But if once we lose this light,
'Tis with us perpetual night.
Why should we defer our joys?
Fame and rumour are but toys.
Cannot we delude the eyes
Of a few poor household spies?
Or his easier ears beguile,
Thus removed by our wile?
'Tis no sin love's fruits to steal,
But the sweet thefts to reveal;
To be taken, to be seen,
These have crimes accounted been.

From BEN JONSON'S *The Description of the Masque, with the Nuptial Songs, celebrating the happy marriage of John, Lord Ramsay, with the Lady Elizabeth Radcliffe,* 1608.

EPITHALAMION.

UP! youths and virgins! up, and praise
The God whose nights outshine his days!
Hymen, whose hallowed rites
Could never boast of brighter lights;
Whose bands pass liberty.
Two of your troop, that with the morn were free,
    Are now waged to his war;
      . And what they are,
      If you'll perfection see,
        Yourselves must be.
Shine, Hesperus! shine forth, thou wished star!

What joy or honours can compare
With holy nuptials, when they are
    Made out of equal parts
Of years, of states, of hands, of hearts;
    When in the happy choice
The spouse and spoused have the foremost voice!
    Such, glad of Hymen's war,
      Live what they are
      And long perfection see:
        And such ours be.
Shine, Hesperus! shine forth, thou wished star!

The solemn state of this one night
Were fit to last an age's light;
   But there are rites behind
Have less of state and more of kind:
Love's wealthy crop of kisses,
And fruitful harvest of his mother's blisses.
   Sound then to Hymen's war!
   That what these are,
   Who will perfection see
   May haste to be.
Shine, Hesperus! shine forth, thou wished star!

Love's Commonwealth consists of toys;
His Council are those antic boys,
   Games, Laughter, Sports, Delights,
That triumph with him on these nights:
   To whom we must give way,
For now their reign begins, and lasts till day.
   They sweeten Hymen's war,
   And in that jar
   Make all, that married be,
   Perfection see.
Shine, Hesperus! shine forth, thou wished star!

Why stays the bridegroom to invade
Her that would be a matron made?
   Good-night! whilst yet we may
Good-night to you a virgin say.
   To-morrow rise the same

Your mother is, and use a nobler name!
    Speed well in Hymen's war,
        That what you are,
        By your perfection, we
        And all may see!
Shine, Hesperus! shine forth, thou wished star!

    To-night is Venus' vigil kept,
    This night no bridegroom ever slept;
        And if the fair bride do,
    The married say 'tis his fault too.
        Wake then, and let your lights
Wake too, for they'll tell nothing of your nights,
        But that in Hymen's war
            You perfect are;
        And such perfection we
            Do pray should be.
Shine, Hesperus! shine forth, thou wished star!

    That, ere the rosy-fingered Morn
    Behold nine moons, there may be born
        A babe to uphold the fame
    Of Radcliffe's blood and Ramsay's name;
        That may, in his great seed,
Wear the long honours of his father's deed.
        Such fruits of Hymen's war
            Most perfect are:
        And all perfection we
            Wish you should see.
Shine, Hesperus! shine forth, thou wished star!

F

From BEN JONSON'S *Epicœne, or the Silent Woman*, 1609.

SIMPLEX MUNDITIIS.

STILL to be neat, still to be drest,
　As you were going to a feast;
Still to be powdered, still perfumed:
Lady, it is to be presumed,
Though art's hid causes are not found,
All is not sweet, all is not sound.

Give me a look, give me a face,
That makes simplicity a grace;
Robes loosely flowing, hair as free:
Such sweet neglect more taketh me
Than all the adulteries of art;
They strike mine eyes, but not my heart.

From BEN JONSON'S *The Masque of Queens*, 1609.

THE WITCHES' SABBATH.

1 *Charm.*　DAME, dame! the watch is set:
　　　Quickly come, we all are met.
From the lakes and from the fens,
From the rocks and from the dens,
From the woods and from the caves,
From the churchyards, from the graves,
From the dungeon, from the tree
That they die on, here are we!
　　　[*Comes she not yet?*
　　　Strike another heat!]

2 *Charm.* The weather is fair, the wind is good :
Up, dame, on your horse of wood !
Or else tuck up your gray frock,
And saddle your goat or your green cock,
And make his bridle a bottom [1] of thread
To roll up how many miles you have rid.
Quickly come away,
For we all stay.
                [Nor yet? nay then
                We'll try her again.]

3 *Charm.* The owl is abroad, the bat, and the toad,
    And so is the cat-a-mountain ; [2]
    The ant and the mole sit both in a hole,
    And the frog peeps out o' the fountain.
The dogs they do bay, and the timbrels play,
    The spindle is now a-turning ;
The moon it is red, and the stars are fled,
    But all the sky is a-burning :
The ditch is made, and our nails the spade,
With pictures full, of wax and of wool :
Their livers I stick with needles quick ;
There lacks but the blood to make up the flood.
Quickly, dame, then bring your part in !
Spur, spur upon little Martin !
Merrily, merrily, make him sail,
A worm in his mouth and a thorn in his tail,
Fire above, and fire below,
With a whip in your hand to make him go !
                [O now she's come !
                Let all be dumb.]

---

[1] Ball of thread.   [2] Wild cat.

From BEN JONSON'S *Masque of Oberon*,[1] 1640.

BUZZ AND HUM.

BUZZ! quoth the Blue-Fly,
  Hum! quoth the Bee;
Buzz and hum! they cry,
  And so do we.
In his ear.! in his nose!
  Thus,—do you see?
He eat the Dormouse——
  Else it was he.

From BEN JONSON'S *The Devil is an Ass*,[2] 1631.

SO WHITE, SO SOFT, SO SWEET, IS SHE!

SEE the chariot at hand here of Love,
  Wherein my Lady rideth!
Each that draws is a swan or a dove,
  And well the car Love guideth.
As she goes, all hearts do duty
    Unto her beauty;
And enamoured do wish, so they might
    But enjoy such a sight,
That they still were to run by her side,
Through swords, through seas, whither she would
    glide.

---

[1] Performed on New Year's Day, 1611.
[2] Acted in 1616. In the play only the second and third stanzas are given; the opening stanza first appeared in "Underwoods."

Do but look on her eyes, they do light
    All that Love's world compriseth !
Do but look on her hair, it is bright
    As Love's star when it riseth !
Do but mark, her forehead's smoother
              Than words that soothe her ;
And from her arched brows such a grace
              Sheds itself through the face,
As alone there triumphs to the life
All the gain, all the good of the elements' strife.

Have you seen but a bright lily grow
    Before rude hands have touched it ?
Have you marked but the fall of the snow
    Before the soil hath smutched it ?
Have you felt the wool of the beaver,
              Or swan's down ever ?
Or have smelt o' the bud of the brier,
              Or the nard in the fire ?
Or have tasted the bag of the bee ?
O so white, O so soft, O so sweet is she !

From BEN JONSON'S *The Vision of Delight*, 1641.[1]

EPILOGUE SPOKEN BY AURORA.

I WAS not wearier where I lay
  By frozen Tithon's side to-night,
Than I am willing now to stay
And be a part of your delight ;
But I am urged by the Day,
Against my will, to bid you come away.

From BEN JONSON'S *Neptune's Triumph for the Return of Albion* [1624].[2]

SPRING ALL THE GRACES OF THE AGE.

SPRING all the Graces of the age,
  And all the Loves of time ;
Bring all the pleasures of the stage,
And relishes of rhyme ;
And all the softnesses of courts,
The looks, the laughters, and the sports :
And mingle all their sweets and salts
That none may say the Triumph halts.

---

[1] Performed at Christmas, 1617.
[2] Rehearsed (but not performed) in January, 1623-4.

PROTEUS, PORTUNUS, AND SARON, THEIR SONG
TO THE LADIES.

Pro. COME, noble nymphs, and do not hide
The joys for which you so provide.
Sar. If not to mingle with the men,
What do you here? Go home again.
Por. Your dressings do confess,
By what we see so curious parts
Of Pallas and Arachne's arts,
That you could mean no less.
Pro. Why do you wear the silk-worm's toils,
Or glory in the shellfish' spoils,
Or strive to show the grains of ore,
That you have gathered on the shore,
Whereof to make a stock
To graft the greener emerald on,
Or any better-watered stone?
Sar. Or ruby of the rock?
Pro. Why do you smell of amber-grise,
Of which was formed Neptune's niece,
The Queen of Love, unless you can,
Like sea-born Venus, love a man?
Sar. Try, pull yourselves unto 't.
Chorus. Your looks, your smiles, and thoughts that meet,
Ambrosian hands, and silver feet,
Do promise you will do 't.

From BEN JONSON'S *Pan's Anniversary*, 1641.[1]

THE SHEPHERD'S HOLYDAY.

1 *Nymph*. THUS, thus begin the yearly rites
Are due to Pan on these bright nights;
His morn now riseth and invites
To sports, to dances, and delights:
All envious and profane, away,
This is the shepherd's holyday.

2 *Nymph*. Strew, strew the glad and smiling ground
With every flower, yet not confound;
The primrose drop, the spring's own spouse,
Bright day's-eyes and the lips of cows;
The garden-star, the queen of May,
The rose, to crown the holyday.

3 *Nymph*. Drop, drop, you violets; change your hues,
Now red, now pale, as lovers use;
And in your death go out as well
As when you lived unto the smell:
That from your odour all may say,
This is the shepherd's holyday.

[1] Performed in 1624 or 1625.

HYMN TO PAN.

1 Nymph.   OF Pan we sing, the best of singers, Pan,
          That taught us swains how first to tune our lays,
         And on the pipe more airs than Phœbus can.
Chorus.   Hear, O you groves, and hills resound his praise.

2 Nymph. Of Pan we sing, the best of leaders, Pan,
          That leads the Naiads and the Dryads forth;
         And to their dances more than Hermes can.
Chorus.   Hear, O you groves, and hills resound his worth.

3 Nymph. Of Pan we sing, the best of hunters, Pan,
          That drives the hart to seek unused ways,
         And in the chase more than Silvanus can.
Chorus.   Hear, O you groves, and hills resound his praise.

2 Nymph. Of Pan we sing, the best of shepherds, Pan,
          That keeps our flocks and us, and both leads forth
         To better pastures than great Pales can.
Chorus.   Hear, O you groves, and hills resound his worth.
         And while his powers and praises thus we sing,
         The valleys let rebound and all the rivers ring.

From BEN JONSON'S *The New Inn*, 1631.

PERFECT BEAUTY.

IT was a beauty that I saw
  So pure, so perfect, as the frame
  Of all the universe was lame,
To that one figure, could I draw,
Or give least line of it a law!
  A skein of silk without a knot,
A fair march made without a halt,
A curious form without a fault,
  A printed book without a blot,
  All beauty, and without a spot!

From BEN JONSON'S *Sad Shepherd*, 1641.

LOVE AND DEATH.

THOUGH I am young and cannot tell
  Either what Death or Love is well,
Yet I have heard they both bear darts,
And both do aim at human hearts;
And then again, I have been told,
Love wounds with heat, as Death with cold;
So that I fear they do but bring
Extremes to touch, and mean one thing.
As in a ruin we it call
One thing to be blown up, or fall;
Or to our end like way may have
By a flash of lightning, or a wave:
So Love's inflamed shaft or brand,
May kill as soon as Death's cold hand;
Except Love's fires the virtue have
To fright the frost out of the grave.

From SAMUEL DANIEL'S *Tethys' Festival*, 1610.

EIDOLA.

ARE they shadows that we see?
And can shadows pleasure give?
Pleasures only shadows be,
Cast by bodies we conceive,
And are made the things we deem
In those figures which they seem.

But these pleasures vanish fast
Which by shadows are exprest.
Pleasures are not if they last;
In their passage is their best:
Glory is most bright and gay
In a flash, and so away.

Feed apace then, greedy eyes,
On the wonder you behold:
Take it sudden as it flies,
Though you take it not to hold:
When your eyes have done their part,
Thought must length it in the heart.

From SAMUEL DANIEL'S *Hymen's Triumph*, 1615.

NOW WHAT IS LOVE?

LOVE is a sickness full of woes,
   All remedies refusing ;
A plant that with most cutting grows,
   Most barren with best using.
        Why so?
More we enjoy it, more it dies ;
If not enjoyed, it sighing cries,
        Heigh ho !
Love is a torment of the mind,
   A tempest everlasting ;
And Jove hath made it of a kind
   Not well, nor full, nor fasting.
        Why so?
More we enjoy it, more it dies ;
If not enjoyed, it sighing cries,
        Heigh ho !

EYES, HIDE MY LOVE.

EYES, hide my love, and do not show
   To any but to her my notes,
Who only doth that cipher know
   Wherewith we pass our secret thoughts :
Belie your looks in others' sight,
And wrong yourselves to do her right.

From THOMAS DEKKER'S *The Shoemaker's Holiday, or the Gentle Craft*, 1600.

THE MERRY MONTH OF MAY.

O, THE month of May, the merry month of May,
So frolic, so gay, and so green, so green, so green!
O, and then did I unto my true love say,
Sweet Peg, thou shalt be my Summer's Queen.

Now the nightingale, the pretty nightingale,
The sweetest singer in all the forest quire,
Entreats thee, sweet Peggy, to hear thy true love's tale :
Lo, yonder she sitteth, her breast against a brier.

But O, I spy the cuckoo, the cuckoo, the cuckoo ;
See where she sitteth ; come away, my joy :
Come away, I prithee, I do not like the cuckoo
Should sing where my Peggy and I kiss and toy.

O, the month of May, the merry month of May,
So frolic, so gay, and so green, so green, so green ;
And then did I unto my true love say,
Sweet Peg, thou shalt be my Summer's Queen.

TROLL THE BOWL!

COLD'S the wind, and wet's the rain,
    Saint Hugh be our good speed!
Ill is the weather that bringeth no gain,
    Nor helps good hearts in need.

Troll the bowl, the jolly nut-brown bowl,
    And here, kind mate, to thee!
Let's sing a dirge for Saint Hugh's soul,
    And down it merrily.

Down-a-down, hey, down-a-down,
    Hey derry derry down-a-down!
Ho! well done, to me let come,
    Ring compass, gentle joy!

Troll the bowl, the nut-brown bowl,
    And here kind, &c. (*as often as there be men to drink*).

At last, when all have drunk, this verse.
Cold's the wind, and wet's the rain,
    Saint Hugh be our good speed!
Ill is the weather that bringeth no gain,
    Nor helps good hearts in need.

From THOMAS DEKKER'S *The Pleasant Comedy of Old Fortunatus*, 1600.

FORTUNE SMILES.

FORTUNE smiles, cry holyday!
Dimples on her cheeks do dwell.
Fortune frowns, cry well-a-day!
Her love is heaven, her hate is hell.
Since heaven and hell obey her power,
Tremble when her eyes do lower:
Since heaven and hell her power obey,
When she smiles cry holyday!
   Holyday with joy we cry,
   And bend, and bend, and merrily
   Sing hymns to Fortune's deity,
   Sing hymns to Fortune's deity.

All.   Let us sing merrily, merrily, merrily!
   With our song let heaven resound,
   Fortune's hands our heads have crowned:
   Let us sing merrily, merrily, merrily!

From *The pleasant Comedy of
Patient Grissell*,[1] 1603.

O, SWEET CONTENT!

ART thou poor, yet hast thou golden slumbers?
    O, sweet content!
Art thou rich, yet is thy mind perplexed?
    O, punishment!
Dost thou laugh to see how fools are vexed
To add to golden numbers golden numbers?
    O, sweet content! O, sweet, &c.

Work apace, apace, apace, apace;
Honest labour bears a lovely face;
Then hey noney, noney, hey noney, noney!

Canst drink the waters of the crisped spring?
    O, sweet content!
Swim'st thou in wealth, yet sink'st in thine own tears?
    O, punishment!
Then he that patiently want's burden bears,
No burden bears, but is a king, a king!
    O, sweet content! &c.
        Work apace, apace, &c.

---

[1] By Dekker, Chettle, and Haughton. Doubtless the songs are by Dekker.

LULLABY.

GOLDEN slumbers kiss your eyes,
Smiles awake you when you rise.
Sleep, pretty wantons, do not cry,
And I will sing a lullaby:
Rock them, rock them, lullaby.

Care is heavy, therefore sleep you;
You are care, and care must keep you.
Sleep, pretty wantons, do not cry,
And I will sing a lullaby:
Rock them, rock them, lullaby.

BEAUTY, ARISE!

BEAUTY, arise, show forth thy glorious shining;
Thine eyes feed love, for them he standeth pining;
Honour and youth attend to do their duty
To thee, their only sovereign beauty.
Beauty, arise, whilst we, thy servants, sing
Io to Hymen, wedlock's jocund king.
  Io to Hymen, Io, Io, sing,
  Of wedlock, love, and youth, is Hymen king.

Beauty, arise, thy glorious lights display,
Whilst we sing Io, glad to see this day.
  Io, Io, to Hymen, Io, Io, sing,
  Of wedlock, love, and youth, is Hymen king.

From Ford and Dekker's *The Sun's Darling*, 1656.[1]

THE INVITATION.

LIVE with me still, and all the measures
    Played to by the spheres I'll teach thee;
Let's but thus dally, all the pleasures
    The moon beholds, her man shall reach thee.

Dwell in mine arms, aloft we'll hover,
    And see fields of armies fighting:
Oh, part not from me! I'll discover
    There all but [?] books of fancy's writing.

Be but my darling, age to free thee
    From her curse, shall fall a-dying;
Call me thy[2] empress, Time to see thee
    Shall forget his art of flying.

HERE LIES THE BLITHE SPRING.

HERE lies the blithe Spring,
    Who first taught birds to sing,
Yet in April herself fell a-crying:
    Then May growing hot,
    A sweating sickness she got,
And the first of June lay a-dying.

[1] Licensed in March, 1623-4. The songs are doubtless by Dekker.
[2] Old ed. "their."

Yet no month can say,
But her merry daughter May
Stuck her coffins with flowers great plenty :
The cuckoo sung in verse
An epitaph o'er her hearse,
But assure you the lines were not dainty.

COUNTRY GLEE.

HAYMAKERS, rakers, reapers, and mowers,
Wait on your Summer-queen ;
Dress up with musk-rose her eglantine bowers,
Daffodils strew the green ;
Sing, dance, and play,
'Tis holiday ;
The sun does bravely shine
On our ears of corn.
Rich as a pearl
Comes every girl,
This is mine, this is mine, this is mine ;
Let us die, ere away they be borne.

Bow to the Sun, to our queen, and that fair one
Come to behold our sports :
Each bonny lass here is counted a rare one,
As those in a prince's courts.
These and we
With country glee,
Will teach the woods to resound,
And the hills with echoes hollow :
Skipping lambs
Their bleating dams,
'Mongst kids shall trip it round ;
For joy thus our wenches we follow.

Wind, jolly huntsmen, your neat bugles shrilly,
   Hounds make a lusty cry;
Spring up, you falconers, the partridges freely,
   Then let your brave hawks fly.
      Horses amain,
      Over ridge, over plain,
The dogs have the stag in chase :
'Tis a sport to content a king.
      So ho ho! through the skies
      How the proud bird flies,
And sousing[1] kills with a grace !
Now the deer falls ; hark, how they ring !

CAST AWAY CARE!

CAST away care ! he that loves sorrow
   Lengthens not a day, nor can buy to-morrow ;
Money is trash ; and he that will spend it,
Let him drink merrily, Fortune will send it.
   Merrily, merrily, merrily, oh, ho !
   Play it off stiffly, we may not part so.

Wine is a charm, it heats the blood too,
Cowards it will arm, if the wine be good too ;
Quickens the wit, and makes the back able,
Scorns to submit to the watch or constable.
         Merrily, &c.

Pots fly about, give us more liquor,
Brothers of a rout, our brains will flow quicker ;
Empty the cask ; score up, we care not ;
Fill all the pots again ; drink on and spare not.
         Merrily, &c.

---

[1] Swooping down on its prey.

From THOMAS DEKKER'S *London's Tempe, or the Field of Happiness*, 1629.

SONG OF THE CYCLOPS.

BRAVE iron, brave hammer, from your sound
The art of music has her ground;
On the anvil thou keep'st time,
Thy knick-a-knock is a smith's best chime.
 Yet thwick-a-thwack, thwick, thwack-a-thwack, thwack,
 Make our brawny sinews crack:
 Then pit-a-pat, pat, pit-a-pat, pat,
 Till thickest bars be beaten flat.

We shoe the horses of the sun,
Harness the dragons of the moon;
Forge Cupid's quiver, bow, and arrows,
And our dame's coach that's drawn with sparrows.
 Till thwick-a-thwack, &c.

Jove's roaring cannons and his rammers
We beat out with our Lemnian hammers;
Mars his gauntlet, helm, and spear,
And Gorgon shield are all made here.
 Till thwick-a-thwack, &c.

The grate which, shut, the day outbars,
Those golden studs which nail the stars,
The globe's case and the axle-tree,
Who can hammer these but we?
 Till thwick-a-thwack, &c.

A warming-pan to heat earth's bed,
Lying i' th' frozen zone half-dead ;
Hob-nails to serve the man i' th' moon,
And sparrowbills [1] to clout Pan's shoon,
    Whose work but ours?
    Till thwick-a-thwack, &c.

Venus' kettles, pots, and pans
We make, or else she brawls and bans ;
Tongs, shovels, andirons [2] have their places,
Else she scratches all our faces.
    Till thwick-a-thwack, &c.

From MUNDAY and CHETTLE'S
Death of Robin Hood, 1601.

ROBIN HOOD BORNE ON HIS BIER.

WEEP, weep, ye woodmen ! wail ;
    Your hands with sorrow wring !
Your master Robin Hood lies dead,
    Therefore sigh as you sing.

Here lie his primer and his beads,
    His bent bow and his arrows keen,
His good sword and his holy cross :
    Now cast on flowers fresh and green.

And, as they fall, shed tears and say
    Well, well-a-day ! well, well-a-day !
Thus cast ye flowers fresh, and sing,
    And on to Wakefield take your way.

---

[1] Shoemakers' nails.   [2] Ornamental fire-irons.

From ANTHONY MUNDAY'S *Metropolis Coronata, the Triumphs of Ancient Drapery*, 1615.

THE SONG OF ROBIN HOOD AND HIS HUNTSMEN.

NOW wend we together, my merry men all,
    Unto the forest side-a:
And there to strike a buck or a doe
    Let our cunning all be tried-a.

Then go we merrily, merrily on,
    To the greenwood to take our stand,
Where we will lie in wait for our game,
    With our bent bows all in our hand.

What life is there like to Robin Hood?
    It is so pleasant a thing-a:
In merry Sherwood he spends his days
    As pleasantly as a king-a.

No man may compare with Robin Hood,
    With Robin Hood, Scathlock and John:
Their like was never, and never will be,
    If in case that they were gone.

They will not away from merry Sherwood
    In any place else to dwell;
For there is neither city nor town
    That likes them half so well.

Our lives are wholly given to hunt,
    And haunt the merry green wood,
Where our best service is daily spent
    For our master Robin Hood.

THOMAS CAMPION.

> From THOMAS CAMPION'S *Description of a Masque presented in honour of the Lord Hayes and his Bride*, 1607.

STROW ABOUT, STROW ABOUT.

NOW hath Flora robbed her bowers
To befriend this place with flowers :
   Strow about, strow about !
The sky rained never kindlier showers.
Flowers with bridals well agree,
Fresh as brides and bridegrooms be :
   Strow about, strow about !
And mix them with fit melody.
Earth hath no princelier flowers
Than roses white and roses red,
But they must still be mingled :
And as a rose new plucked from Venus' thorn,
So doth a bride her bridegroom's bed adorn.

Divers divers flowers affect
For some private dear respect :
   Strow about, strow about !
Let every one his own affect ;
But he's none of Flora's friend
That will not the rose commend.
   Strow about, strow about !
Let princes princely flowers defend :
Roses, the garden's pride,
Are flowers for love and flowers for kings,
In courts desired and weddings :
And as a rose in Venus' bosom worn,
So doth a bridegroom his bride's bed adorn.

From Francis Beaumont's *The Masque of the Inner Temple*, performed February, 1612-3.[1]

SONG FOR A DANCE.

SHAKE off your heavy trance!
 And leap into a dance
Such as no mortals use to tread :
 Fit only for Apollo
To play to, for the moon to lead,
 And all the stars to follow!

THE MASQUERS CALLED AWAY.

YE should stay longer if we durst :
 Away! Alas that he that first
Gave Time wild wings to fly away—
Hath now no power to make him stay!
And though these games[2] must needs be played,
I would this pair, when they are laid,
 And not a creature nigh 'em,
Could catch his scythe, as he doth pass,
And clip his wings, and break his glass,
 And keep him ever by 'em.

---

[1] In honour of the marriage of the Count Palatine with the Princess Elizabeth.
[2] "Then loud music sounds, supposed to call them to their Olympian games."

THE BRIDAL SONG.

PEACE and silence be the guide
    To the man and to the bride!
If there be a joy yet new
In marriage, let it fall on you,
    That all the world may wonder!
If we should stay, we should do worse,
And turn our blessing to a curse
    By keeping you asunder.

> From BEAUMONT and FLET-
> CHER'S *The Woman-Hater*,
> 1607.

COME, SLEEP.

COME, Sleep, and with thy sweet deceiving,
    Lock me in delight awhile;
    Let some pleasing dreams beguile
    All my fancies; that from thence
    I may feel an influence,
All my powers of care bereaving!

Though but a shadow, but a sliding,
    Let me know some little joy!
    We that suffer long annoy
    Are contented with a thought,
    Through an idle fancy wrought:
Oh, let my joys have some abiding!

From BEAUMONT and FLETCHER'S *The Knight of the Burning Pestle*, 1613.[1]

NO MEDICINE TO MIRTH.

'TIS mirth that fills the veins with blood,
  More than wine, or sleep, or food;
Let each man keep his heart at ease;
No man dies of that disease.
He that would his body keep
From diseases, must not weep;
But whoever laughs and sings,
Never he his body brings
Into fevers, gouts, or rheums,
Or lingeringly his lungs consumes;
Or meets with aches[2] in his bone,
Or catarrhs, or griping stone:
But contented lives for aye;
The more he laughs, the more he may.

COME, YOU WHOSE LOVES ARE DEAD.

COME, you whose loves are dead,
    And, whiles I sing,
    Weep, and wring
Every hand, and every head
Bind with cypress and sad yew;
Ribbons black and candles blue
For him that was of men most true!

[1] Produced in 1610-11.   [2] A dissyllable.

Come with heavy moaning,
   And on his grave
   Let him have
Sacrifice of sighs and groaning;
Let him have fair flowers enow,
White and purple, green and yellow,
For him that was of men most true!

RALPH, THE MAY-LORD.

LONDON, to thee I do present
   The merry month of May;
Let each true subject be content
   To hear me what I say:
For from the top of conduit-head,
   As plainly may appear,
I will both tell my name to you,
   And wherefore I came here.
My name is Ralph, by due descent,
   Though not ignoble I,
Yet far inferior to the flock
   Of gracious grocery;
And by the common counsel of
   My fellows in the Strand,
With gilded staff and crossed scarf,
   The May-lord here I stand.
Rejoice, oh, English hearts, rejoice!
   Rejoice, oh, lovers dear!
Rejoice, oh, city, town, and country,
   Rejoice eke every shire![1]

[1] To be pronounced (as frequently) "shere."

For now the fragrant flowers do spring
   And sprout in seemly sort,
The little birds do sit and sing,
   The lambs do make fine sport;
And now the birchen-tree doth bud,
   That makes the schoolboy cry;
The morris rings, while hobby-horse
   Doth foot it feateously;
The lords and ladies now abroad,
   For their disport and play,
Do kiss sometimes upon the grass,
   And sometimes in the hay.
Now butter with a leaf of sage
   Is good to purge the blood;
Fly Venus and phlebotomy,
   For they are neither good!
Now little fish on tender stone
   Begin to cast their bellies,
And sluggish snails, that erst were mewed,
   Do creep out of their shellies;
The rumbling rivers now do warm,
   For little boys to paddle;
The sturdy steed now goes to grass,
   And up they hang his saddle;
The heavy hart, the bellowing buck,
   The rascal,[1] and the pricket,[2]
Are now among the yeoman's pease,
   And leave the fearful thicket;
And be like them, oh, you, I say,
   Of this same noble town,

---

[1] A lean deer.   [2] A buck in his second year.

And lift aloft your velvet heads,
    And slipping off your gown,
With bells[1] on legs, and napkins clean
    Unto your shoulders tied,
With scarfs and garters as you please,
    And "Hey for our town!"[2] cried,
March out, and show your willing minds,
    By twenty and by twenty,
To Hogsdon,[2] or to Newington,
    Where ale and cakes are plenty;
And let it ne'er be said for shame,
    That we the youths of London
Lay thrumming of our caps at home,
    And left our custom undone.
Up then, I say, both young and old,
    Both man and maid a-maying,
With drums and guns that bounce aloud,
    And merry tabor playing!
Which to prolong, God save our king,
    And send his country peace,
And root out treason from the land!
    And so, my friends, I cease.

---

[1] "With bells," &c.—the trappings of the morris-dancers.
[2] See *Notes* at the end of the volume.

From BEAUMONT and FLETCHER'S *Cupid's Revenge*, 1615.[1]

AT THE TEMPLE OF CUPID.

Priest. COME, my children, let your feet
In an even measure meet,
And your cheerful voices rise,
To present this sacrifice
To great Cupid, in whose name,
I his priest begin the same.
Young men, take your loves and kiss;
Thus our Cupid honoured is;
Kiss again, and in your kissing
Let no promises be missing;
Nor let any maiden here
Dare to turn away her ear
Unto the whisper of her love,
But give bracelet, ring, or glove,
As a token to her sweeting,
Of an after secret meeting.
Now, boy, sing, to stick our hearts
Fuller of great Cupid's darts.

[1] Performed on the Sunday following New Year's night, 1611-12.

THE SONG.

LOVERS, rejoice! your pains shall be rewarded,
　The god of love himself grieves at your crying;
No more shall frozen honour be regarded,
Nor the coy faces of a maid denying.
No more shall virgins sigh, and say "We dare not,
For men are false, and what they do they care not."
All shall be well again; then do not grieve;
Men shall be true, and women shall believe.

Lovers, rejoice! what you shall say henceforth,
When you have caught your sweethearts in your arms,
It shall be accounted oracle and worth;
No more faint-hearted girls shall dream of harms,
And cry "They are too young"; the god hath said,
Fifteen shall make a mother of a maid:
Then, wise men, pull your roses yet unblown:
Love hates the too-ripe fruit that falls alone.

CUPID, PARDON WHAT IS PAST.

CUPID, pardon what is past,
And forgive our sins at last!
Then we will be coy no more,
But thy deity adore;
Troths at fifteen we will plight,
And will tread a dance each night,
In the fields, or by the fire,
With the youths that have desire.
Given ear-rings we will wear,
Bracelets of our lovers' hair,
Which they on our arms shall twist,
With their names carved, on our wrist;
All the money that we owe [1]
We in tokens will bestow;
And learn to write that, when 'tis sent,
Only our loves know what is meant.
Oh, then pardon what is past,
And forgive our sins at last!

[1] Own.

From BEAUMONT and FLETCHER'S *The Maid's Tragedy*, 1619.[1]

BRIDAL SONGS.

FIRST SONG, *during which Proteus and other sea-deities enter.*

CYNTHIA, to thy power and thee
           We obey.
Joy to this great company!
           And no day
Come to steal this night away,
    Till the rites of love are ended,
And the lusty bridegroom say,
    Welcome, light, of all befriended!

Pace out, you watery powers below;
           Let your feet,
Like the galleys when they row,
           Even beat;
Let your unknown measures, set
    To the still winds, tell to all
That gods are come, immortal, great,
    To honour this great nuptial.

[1] Produced not later than 1611.

SECOND SONG.

HOLD back thy hours, dark Night, till we have done;
    The Day will come too soon;
Young maids will curse thee, if thou steal'st away
And leav'st their losses open to the day:
    Stay, stay, and hide
    The blushes of the bride.

Stay, gentle Night, and with thy darkness cover
    The kisses of her lover;
Stay, and confound her tears and her shrill cryings,
Her weak denials, vows, and often-dyings;
    Stay, and hide all:
    But help not, though she call.

THIRD SONG.

TO bed, to bed! Come, Hymen, lead the bride,
    And lay her by her husband's side;
      Bring in the virgins every one
      That grieve to lie alone,
That they may kiss while they may say a maid;
To-morrow 'twill be other kissed and said.
      Hesperus, be long a-shining,
      While these lovers are a-twining.

ASPATIA'S SONG.

Lay a garland on my hearse
 Of the dismal yew;
Maidens, willow branches bear;
 Say, I died true.

My love was false, but I was firm
 From my hour of birth.
Upon my buried body lie
 Lightly, gentle earth!

FICKLENESS.

I could never have the power
 To love one above an hour,
But my head would prompt mine eye
 On some other man to fly.
Venus, fix thou mine eyes fast,
Or, if not, give me all that I shall see at last.

From JOHN FLETCHER'S *The Faithful Shepherdess*, n.d. [1609-10.]

THE SATYR AND CLORIN.

THROUGH yon same bending plain
  That flings his arms down to the main,
And through these thick woods have I run,
Whose bottom never kissed the sun
Since the lusty spring began;
All to please my Master Pan,
Have I trotted without rest
To get him fruit; for at a feast
He entertains, this coming night,
His paramour, the Syrinx bright.
But, behold a fairer sight!
By that heavenly form of thine,
Brightest fair, thou art divine,
Sprung from great immortal race
Of the gods; for in thy face
Shines more awful majesty,
Than dull weak mortality
Dare with misty eyes behold,
And live: therefore on this mould
Lowly do I bend my knee
In worship of thy deity.
Deign it, goddess, from my hand,
To receive whate'er this land
From her fertile womb doth send
Of her choice fruits; and but lend

Belief to that the Satyr tells:
Fairer by the famous wells
To this present day ne'er grew,
Never better nor more true.
Here be grapes, whose lusty blood
Is the learned poet's good,
Sweeter yet did never crown
The head of Bacchus; nuts more brown
Than the squirrel's teeth that crack them;
Deign, oh fairest fair, to take them!
For these black-eyed Dryope
Hath often-times commanded me
With my clasped knee to climb:
See how well the lusty time
Hath decked their rising cheeks in red,
Such as on your lips is spread!
Here be berries for a queen,
Some be red, some be green;
These are of that luscious meat,
The great god Pan himself doth eat:
All these, and what the woods can yield,
The hanging mountain, or the field,
I freely offer, and ere long
Will bring you more, more sweet and strong;
Till when, humbly leave I take,
Lest the great Pan do awake,
That sleeping lies in a deep glade,
Under a broad beech's shade.
I must go, I must run
Swifter than the fiery sun.

GREAT GOD PAN.

SING his praises that doth keep
    Our flocks from harm,
Pan, the father of our sheep;
    And arm in arm
Tread we softly in a round,
Whilst the hollow neighbouring ground
Fills the music with her sound.

Pan, oh, great god Pan, to thee
    Thus do we sing!
Thou that keep'st us chaste and free
    As the young spring;
Ever be thy honour spoke,
From that place the morn is broke,
To that place day doth unyoke!

THE WANTON SHEPHERDESS.

COME, shepherds, come!
    Come away
    Without delay,
Whilst the gentle time doth stay.
  Green woods are dumb,
And will never tell to any
Those dear kisses, and those many
Sweet embraces, that are given;
Dainty pleasures, that would even
Raise in coldest age a fire,
And give virgin-blood desire.
    Then, if ever,
    Now or never,
    Come and have it:
    Think not I
    Dare deny,
    If you crave it.

THE EVENING KNELL.

SHEPHERDS all, and maidens fair,
  Fold your flocks up, for the air
'Gins to thicken, and the sun
Already his great course hath run.
See the dew-drops how they kiss
Every little flower that is,
Hanging on their velvet heads,
Like a rope of crystal beads:
See the heavy clouds low falling,
And bright Hesperus down calling
The dead Night from under ground;
At whose rising mists unsound,

Damps and vapours fly apace,
Hovering o'er the wanton face
Of these pastures, where they come,
Striking dead both bud and bloom:
Therefore, from such danger lock
Every one his loved flock;
And let your dogs lie loose without,
Lest the wolf come as a scout
From the mountain, and, ere day,
Bear a lamb or kid away;
Or the crafty thievish fox
Break upon your simple flocks.
To secure yourselves from these,
Be not too secure in ease;
Let one eye his watches keep,
Whilst the t'other eye doth sleep;
So you shall good shepherds prove,
And for ever hold the love
Of our great god. Sweetest slumbers,
And soft silence, fall in numbers
On your eye-lids! So, farewell!
Thus I end my evening's knell.

THE HOLY WELL.

FROM thy forehead thus I take
These herbs, and charge thee not awake
Till in yonder holy well
Thrice, with powerful magic spell,
Filled with many a baleful word,
Thou hast been dipped. Thus, with my cord
Of blasted hemp, by moonlight twined,
I do thy sleepy body bind.

I turn thy head unto the east,
And thy feet unto the west,
Thy left arm to the south put forth,
And thy right unto the north.
I take thy body from the ground,
In this deep and deadly swound,
And into this holy spring
I let thee slide down by my string.
Take this maid, thou holy pit,
To thy bottom; nearer yet;
In thy water pure and sweet,
By thy leave I dip her feet;
Thus I let her lower yet,
That her ankles may be wet;
Yet down lower, let her knee
In thy waters washed be.
There stop. Fly away,
Everything that loves the day.
Truth, that hath but one face,
Thus I charm thee from this place.
Snakes that cast your coats for new,
Chameleons that alter hue,
Hares that yearly sexes change,
Proteus altering oft and strange,
Hecate with shapes three,
Let this maiden changed be,
With this holy water wet,
To the shape of Amoret!
Cynthia, work thou with my charm!
Thus I draw thee free from harm,
Up out of this blessed lake:
Rise both like her and awake!

PAN'S SENTINEL.

NOW, whilst the moon doth rule the sky,
And the stars, whose feeble light
Give a pale shadow to the night,
Are up, great Pan commanded me
To walk this grove about, whilst he,
In a corner of the wood,
Where never mortal foot hath stood,
Keeps dancing, music, and a feast,
To entertain a lovely guest :
Where he gives her many a rose,
Sweeter than the breath that blows
The leaves, grapes, berries of the best ;
I never saw so great a feast.
But, to my charge. Here must I stay,
To see what mortals lose their way,
And by a false fire, seeming bright,
Train them in and leave them right.
Then must I watch if any be
Forcing of a chastity ;
If I find it, then in haste
Give my wreathed horn a blast,
And the fairies all will run,
Wildly dancing by the moon,
And will pinch him to the bone,
Till his lustful thoughts be gone.

Back again about this ground ;
Sure I hear a mortal sound.—

I bind thee by this powerful spell,
By the waters of this well,
By the glimmering moon-beams bright,
Speak again, thou mortal wight!

Here the foolish mortal lies,
Sleeping on the ground. Arise!
The poor wight is almost dead;
On the ground his wounds have bled,
And his clothes fouled with his blood:
To my goddess in the wood
Will I lead him, whose hands pure
Will help this mortal wight to cure.

AMORET AND THE RIVER-GOD.

God. WHAT powerful charms my streams do bring
Back again unto their spring,
With such force, that I their god,
Three times striking with my rod,
Could not keep them in their ranks?
My fishes shoot into the banks;
There's not one that stays and feeds,
All have hid them in the weeds.
Here's a mortal almost dead,
Faln into my river-head,
Hallowed so with many a spell,
That till now none ever fell.
'Tis a female young and clear,
Cast in by some ravisher:
See upon her breast a wound,
On which there is no plaster bound.

Yet she's warm, her pulses beat,
'Tis a sign of life and heat.—
If thou be'st a virgin pure,
I can give a present cure :
Take a drop into thy wound,
From my watery locks, more round
Than orient pearl, and far more pure
Than unchaste flesh may endure.—
See, she pants, and from her flesh
The warm blood gusheth out afresh.
She is an unpolluted maid ;
I must have this bleeding staid.
From my banks I pluck this flower
With holy hand, whose virtuous power
Is at once to heal and draw.—
The blood returns. I never saw
A fairer mortal. Now doth break
Her deadly slumber. Virgin, speak.

Amoret. Who hath restored my sense, given me new breath,
And brought me back out of the arms of death?
God. I have healed thy wounds.
Amoret. Aye me !
God. Fear not him that succoured thee.
I am this fountain's god. Below
My waters to a river grow,
And 'twixt two banks with osiers set,
That only prosper in the wet,
Through the meadows do they glide,
Wheeling still on every side,
Sometimes winding round about,
To find the evenest channel out.
And if thou wilt go with me,

Leaving mortal company,
In the cool streams shalt thou lie,
Free from harm as well as I :
I will give thee for thy food
No fish that useth in the mud ;
But trout and pike, that love to swim
Where the gravel from the brim
Through the pure streams may be seen :
Orient pearl fit for a queen
Will I give, thy love to win,
And a shell to keep them in ;
Not a fish in all my brook
That shall disobey thy look,
But, when thou wilt, come sliding by,
And from thy white hand take a fly :
And to make thee understand
How I can my waves command,
They shall bubble whilst I sing,
Sweeter than the silver string.

The Song.

Do not fear to put thy feet
Naked in the river sweet ;
Think not leech, or newt, or toad,
Will bite thy foot, when thou hast trod ;
Nor let the water rising high,
As thou wad'st in, make thee cry
And sob ; but ever live with me,
And not a wave shall trouble thee !

TO PAN.

ALL ye woods, and trees, and bowers,
All ye virtues and ye powers
That inhabit in the lakes,
In the pleasant springs or brakes,
    Move your feet
      To our sound,
    Whilst we greet
      All this ground
With his honour and his name
That defends our flocks from blame.

He is great, and he is just,
He is ever good, and must
Thus be honoured. Daffadillies,
Roses, pinks, and loved lilies,
    Let us fling,
    Whilst we sing,
    Ever holy,
    Ever holy,
Ever honoured, ever young!
Thus great Pan is ever sung.

THE SATYR'S LEAVE-TAKING.

THOU divinest, fairest, brightest,
Thou most powerful maid, and whitest,
Thou most virtuous and most blessed,
Eyes of stars, and golden-tressed
Like Apollo! tell me, sweetest,
What new service now is meetest

For the Satyr? Shall I stray
In the middle air, and stay
The sailing rack, or nimbly take
Hold by the moon, and gently make
Suit to the pale queen of night
For a beam to give thee light?
Shall I dive into the sea,
And bring thee coral, making way
Through the rising waves that fall
In snowy fleeces? Dearest, shall
I catch thee wanton fawns, or flies
Whose woven wings the summer dyes
Of many colours? get thee fruit,
Or steal from Heaven old Orpheus' lute?
All these I'll venture for, and more,
To do her service all these woods adore.

Holy virgin, I will dance
Round about these woods as quick
As the breaking light, and prick [1]
Down the lawns and down the vales
Faster than the wind-mill sails.
So I take my leave, and pray
All the comforts of the day,
Such as Phœbus' heat doth send
On the earth, may still befriend
Thee and this arbour!

[1] Speed.

From JOHN FLETCHER'S *The Captain*, 1647.[1]

TELL ME, DEAREST, WHAT IS LOVE?

TELL me, dearest, what is love?
'Tis a lightning from above;
'Tis an arrow, 'tis a fire,
'Tis a boy they call Desire.
    'Tis a grave,
    Gapes to have
Those poor fools that long to prove.

Tell me more, are women true?
Yes, some are, and some as you.
    Some are willing, some are strange,[2]
    Since you men first taught to change.
        And till troth
        Be in both,
All shall love, to love anew.

Tell me more yet, can they grieve?
Yes, and sicken sore, but live,
    And be wise, and delay,
    When you men are as wise as they.
        Then I see,
        Faith will be,
Never till they both believe.

---

[1] Produced in 1613.—The play is mainly by Fletcher, but a second author's hand is distinguishable. (We find the first two stanzas of the song, with variations, in *The Knight of the Burning Pestle.*)

[2] Coy.

FAREWELL, FALSE LOVE!

AWAY, delights! go seek some other dwelling,
    For I must die.
Farewell, false love! thy tongue is ever telling
    Lie after lie.
For ever let me rest now from thy smarts;
    Alas, for pity, go,
    And fire their hearts
That have been hard to thee! mine was not so.

Never again deluding love shall know me,
    For I will die;
And all those griefs that think to overgrow me,
    Shall be as I:
For ever will I sleep, while poor maids cry,
    "Alas, for pity, stay,
    And let us die
With thee! men cannot mock us in the clay."

COME HITHER, YOU THAT LOVE.

COME hither, you that love, and hear me sing
    Of joys still growing,
Green, fresh, and lusty as the pride of spring,
    And ever blowing.
Come hither, youths that blush, and dare not know
    What is desire;
And old men, worse than you, that cannot blow
    One spark of fire;
And with the power of my enchanting song,
Boys shall be able men, and old men young.

Come hither, you that hope, and you that cry;
    Leave off complaining;
Youth, strength, and beauty, that shall never die,
    Are here remaining.
Come hither, fools, and blush you stay so long
    From being blessed;
And mad men, worse than you, that suffer wrong,
    Yet seek no rest;
And in an hour, with my enchanting song,
You shall be ever pleased, and young maids long.

From JOHN FLETCHER'S *The Tragedy of Valentinian*, 1647.[1]

LOVE'S EMBLEMS.

NOW the lusty spring is seen;
   Golden yellow, gaudy blue,
Daintily invite the view.
Everywhere on every green,
Roses blushing as they blow,
   And enticing men to pull,
Lilies whiter than the snow,
   Woodbines of sweet honey full:
      All love's emblems, and all cry,
      "Ladies, if not plucked, we die."

Yet the lusty spring hath stayed;
   Blushing red and purest white
   Daintily to love invite
Every woman, every maid.
Cherries kissing as they grow,
   And inviting men to taste,
Apples even ripe below,
   Winding gently to the waist:
      All love's emblems, and all cry,
      "Ladies, if not plucked, we die."

[1] Produced before March, 1618-19.

WHAT THE MIGHTY LOVE HAS DONE.

HEAR, ye ladies that despise,
   What the mighty Love has done;
Fear examples, and be wise:
   Fair Calisto was a nun;
Leda, sailing on the stream
   To deceive the hopes of man,
Love accounting but a dream,
   Doted on a silver swan;
     Danaë, in a brazen tower,
     Where no love was, loved a shower.

Hear, ye ladies that are coy,
   What the mighty Love can do;
Fear the fierceness of the boy:
   The chaste moon he makes to woo;
Vesta, kindling holy fires,
   Circled round about with spies,
Never dreaming loose desires,
   Doting at the altar dies;
     Ilion, in a short hour, higher
     He can build, and once more fire.

CARE-CHARMING SLEEP.

CARE-charming Sleep, thou easer of all woes,
  Brother to Death, sweetly thyself dispose
On this afflicted prince; fall like a cloud,
In gentle showers; give nothing that is loud,
Or painful to his slumbers; easy, light,[1]
And as a purling stream, thou son of Night
Pass by his troubled senses; sing his pain,
Like hollow murmuring wind or silver rain;
Into this prince gently, oh, gently slide,
And kiss him into slumbers like a bride.

GOD LYÆUS, EVER YOUNG.

GOD Lyæus, ever young,
  Ever honoured, ever sung,
Stained with blood of lusty grapes,
In a thousand lusty shapes,
Dance upon the mazer's brim,
In the crimson liquor swim;
From thy plenteous hand divine,
Let a river run with wine:
    God of youth, let this day here
    Enter neither care nor fear.

---

[1] Old eds. "sweet."

From JOHN FLETCHER'S *The Mad Lover*, 1647.[1]

THE LOVER'S HEART.

GO, happy heart ! for thou shalt lie
Intombed in her for whom I die,
Example of her cruelty.

Tell her, if she chance to chide
Me for slowness, in her pride,
That it was for her I died.

If a tear escape her eye,
'Tis not for my memory,
But thy rites of obsequy.

The altar was my loving breast,
My heart the sacrificed beast,
And I was myself the priest.

Your body was the sacred shrine,
Your cruel mind the power divine,
Pleased with hearts of men, not kine.

[1] Produced before March, 1618-19.

ORPHEUS I AM, COME FROM THE DEEPS BELOW.

ORPHEUS I am, come from the deeps below,
To thee, fond man, the plagues of love to show.
To the fair fields where loves eternal dwell
There's none that come, but first they pass through hell:
Hark, and beware! unless thou hast loved, ever
Beloved again, thou shalt see those joys never.

    Hark how they groan that died despairing!
        Oh, take heed, then!
    Hark how they howl for over-daring!
        All these were men.

    They that be fools, and die for fame,
      They lose their name;
      And they that bleed,
      Hark how they speed!

    Now in cold frosts, now scorching fires
    They sit, and curse their lost desires;
Nor shall these souls be free from pains and fears,
Till women waft them over in their tears.

TO VENUS.

OH, fair sweet goddess, queen of loves,
Soft and gentle as thy doves,
Humble-eyed, and ever ruing
Those poor hearts, their loves pursuing !
Oh, thou mother of delights,
Crowner of all happy nights,
Star of dear content and pleasure,
Of mutual loves the endless treasure !
Accept this sacrifice we bring,
Thou continual youth and spring ;
Grant this lady her desires,
And every hour we'll crown thy fires.

ARM, ARM, ARM, ARM !

ARM, arm, arm, arm ! the scouts are all come in ;
Keep your ranks close, and now your honours win.
Behold from yonder hill the foe appears ;
Bows, bills, glaves, arrows, shields, and spears !
Like a dark wood he comes, or tempest pouring ;
Oh, view the wings of horse the meadows scouring !
The van-guard marches bravely.   Hark, the drums !
         Dub, dub!
They meet, they meet, and now the battle comes :
   See how the arrows fly,
   That darken all the sky !
   Hark how the trumpets sound,
   Hark how the hills rebound,
     Tara, tara, tara, tara, tara !

Hark how the horses charge! in, boys, boys, in!
The battle totters; now the wounds begin:
    Oh, how they cry!
    Oh, how they die!
Room for the valiant Memnon, armed with thunder!
  See how he breaks the ranks asunder!
They fly! they fly! Eumenes has the chase,
And brave Polybius makes good his place.
    To the plains, to the woods,
    To the rocks, to the floods,
They fly for succour. Follow, follow, follow!
Hark how the soldiers hollow!
                      Hey, hey!
    Brave Diocles is dead,
    And all his soldiers fled;
    The battle's won, and lost,
    That many a life hath cost.

From JOHN FLETCHER'S *The Humorous Lieutenant*, 1647.[1]

THE LOVE-CHARM.

RISE from the shades below,
    All you that prove
The helps of looser love!
    Rise, and bestow
Upon this cup whatever may compel,
By powerful charm and unresisted spell,
A heart unwarmed to melt in love's desires!
Distil into this liquor all your fires;
    Heats, longings, tears;
    But keep back frozen fears;
That she may know, that has all power defied,
Art is a power that will not be denied.

[1] Produced circ. 1619.

From JOHN FLETCHER'S *Women Pleased*, 1647.[1]

TO HIS SLEEPING MISTRESS.

OH, fair sweet face! oh, eyes, celestial bright,
Twin stars in heaven, that now adorn the night!
Oh, fruitful lips, where cherries ever grow,
And damask cheeks, where all sweet beauties blow!
Oh, thou, from head to foot divinely fair!
Cupid's most cunning net's made of that hair;
And, as he weaves himself for curious eyes,
"Oh me, oh me, I'm caught myself!" he cries:
Sweet rest about thee, sweet and golden sleep,
Soft peaceful thoughts, your hourly watches keep,
Whilst I in wonder sing this sacrifice,
To beauty sacred, and those angel eyes!

A WOMAN WILL HAVE HER WILL.

Question. TELL me, what is that only thing
  For which all women long;
  Yet, having what they most desire,
  To have it does them wrong?
Answer. 'Tis not to be chaste, nor fair,
  (Such gifts malice may impair,)
  Richly trimmed, to walk or ride,
  Or to wanton unespied;
  To preserve an honest name,
  And so to give it up to fame;
  These are toys. In good or ill
  They desire to have their will:
  Yet, when they have it, they abuse it,
  For they know not how to use it.

[1] Produced circ. 1620.

From JOHN FLETCHER'S *The False One*, 1647.[1]

THE MASQUE OF NILUS.

Isis and the Three Labourers.

Isis. ISIS, the goddess of this land,
Bids thee, great Cæsar, understand
And mark our customs: and first know,
With greedy eyes these watch the flow
Of plenteous Nilus; when he comes,
With songs, with dances, timbrels, drums,
They entertain him; cut his way,
And give his proud heads leave to play;
   Nilus himself shall rise, and show
   His matchless wealth in overflow.
Labourers. Come, let us help the reverend Nile;
He's very old; alas, the while!
Let us dig him easy ways,
And prepare a thousand plays:
To delight his streams, let's sing
A loud welcome to our spring;
This way let his curling heads
Fall into our new-made beds;
This way let his wanton spawns
Frisk, and glide it o'er the lawns.
This way profit comes, and gain:
How he tumbles here amain!
How his waters haste to fall
Into our channels! Labour, all,

[1] Produced circ. 1620.

And let him in ; let Nilus flow,
And perpetual plenty show.
With incense let us bless the brim,
And, as the wanton fishes swim,
Let us gums and garlands fling,
And loud our timbrels ring.
   Come, old father, come away !
   Our labour is our holiday.

Enter Nilus.

Isis. Here comes the aged river now,
With garlands of great pearl his brow
Begirt and rounded. In his flow
All things take life, and all things grow :
A thousand wealthy treasures still,
To do him service at his will,
Follow his rising flood, and pour
Perpetual blessings in our store.
Hear him ; and next there will advance
His sacred heads to tread a dance,
In honour of my royal guest :
Mark them too ; and you have a feast.
Nilus. Make room for my rich waters' fall,
    And bless my flood ;
Nilus comes flowing to you all
    Increase and good.
Now the plants and flowers shall spring,
And the merry ploughman sing :
In my hidden waves I bring
Bread, and wine, and every thing.
Let the damsels sing me in,
   Sing aloud, that I may rise :

Your holy feasts and hours begin,
  And each hand bring a sacrifice.
Now my wanton pearls I show,
That to ladies' fair necks grow;
  Now my gold,
And treasures that can ne'er be told,
Shall bless this land, by my rich flow;
And after this, to crown your eyes,
My hidden holy heads arise.

Enter the Seven Heads of Nilus, and dance.
Exeunt Masquers.

From JOHN FLETCHER'S *The
Little French Lawyer*, 1647.[1]

BRIDAL SONG.

COME away! bring on the bride,
  And place her by her lover's side.
You fair troop of maids attend her;
Pure and holy thoughts befriend her.
Blush, and wish, you virgins all,
Many such fair nights may fall.
Hymen, fill the house with joy;
All thy sacred fires employ;
Bless the bed with holy love:
Now, fair orb of beauty, move.

[1] Produced circ. 1620?

SONG IN THE WOOD.

THIS way, this way come, and hear,
You that hold these pleasures dear;
Fill your ears with our sweet sound,
Whilst we melt the frozen ground.
This way come; make haste, oh, fair!
Let your clear eyes gild the air;
Come, and bless us with your sight;
This way, this way, seek delight!

From JOHN FLETCHER'S *Beggars' Bush*, 1647.[1]

THE BEGGARS' HOLIDAY.

CAST our caps and cares away:
This is beggars' holiday!
At the crowning of our king,
Thus we ever dance and sing.
In the world look out and see,
Where so happy a prince as he?
Where the nation live so free,
And so merry as do we?
Be it peace, or be it war,
Here at liberty we are,
And enjoy our ease and rest:
To the field we are not pressed;
Nor are called into the town,
To be troubled with the gown.

[1] Acted in 1622.

Hang all offices, we cry,
And the magistrate too, by !
When the subsidy's increased,
We are not a penny sessed ;
Nor will any go to law
With the beggar for a straw.
All which happiness, he brags,
He doth owe unto his rags.

From John Fletcher's *The Spanish Curate*, 1647.[1]

SPEAK, THOU FAIREST FAIR.

DEAREST, do not you delay me,
    Since, thou knowest, I must be gone ;
Wind and tide, 'tis thought, doth stay me,
    But 'tis wind that must be blown
        From that breath, whose native smell
        Indian odours far excel.

Oh, then speak, thou fairest fair !
    Kill not him that vows to serve thee ;
But perfume this neighbouring air,
    Else dull silence, sure, will sterve me :
        'Tis a word that's quickly spoken,
        Which being restrained, a heart is broken.

---

[1] Acted in 1622.—This song and the next are from the second folio, 1679.

LET THE BELLS RING, AND LET THE BOYS SING.

LET the bells ring, and let the boys sing,
    The young lasses skip and play ;
Let the cups go round, till round goes the ground ;
    Our learned old vicar will stay.

Let the pig turn merrily, merrily, ah !
    And let the fat goose swim ;
For verily, verily, verily, ah !
    Our vicar this day shall be trim.

The stewed cock shall crow, cock-a-loodle-loo,
    A loud cock-a-loodle shall he crow ;
The duck and the drake shall swim in a lake
    Of onions and claret below.

Our wives shall be neat, to bring in our meat
    To thee our most noble adviser ;
Our pains shall be great, and bottles shall sweat,
    And we ourselves will be wiser.

We'll labour and swink,[1] we'll kiss and we'll drink,
    And tithes shall come thicker and thicker ;
We'll fall to our plough, and get children enow,
    And thou shalt be learned old vicar.

[1] Toil.

JOHN FLETCHER.

> From JOHN FLETCHER'S *The Lovers' Progress*, 1647.[1]

THE DEAD HOST'S WELCOME.

'TIS late and cold; stir up the fire;
   Sit close, and draw the table nigher;
Be merry, and drink wine that's old,
A hearty medicine 'gainst a cold:
Your beds of wanton down the best,
Where you shall tumble to your rest;
I could wish you wenches too,
But I am dead, and cannot do.
Call for the best the house may ring,
Sack, white, and claret, let them bring,
And drink apace, while breath you have;
You'll find but cold drink in the grave:
Plover, partridge, for your dinner,
And a capon for the sinner,
You shall find ready when you're up,
And your horse shall have his sup:
Welcome, welcome, shall fly round,
And I shall smile, though under ground.

[1] Produced in 1623?

From John Fletcher's *A Wife for a Month*, 1647.[1]

TO THE BLEST EVANTHE.

LET those complain that feel Love's cruelty,
    And in sad legends write their woes;
With roses gently 'has corrected me,
    My war is without rage or blows:
My mistress' eyes shine fair on my desires,
And hope springs up inflamed with her new fires.

No more an exile will I dwell,
    With folded arms, and sighs all day,
Reckoning the torments of my hell,
    And flinging my sweet joys away:
I am called home again to quiet peace;
My mistress smiles, and all my sorrows cease.

Yet, what is living in her eye,
    Or being blessed with her sweet tongue,
If these no other joys imply?
    A golden gyve, a pleasing wrong:
To be your own but one poor month, I'd give
My youth, my fortune, and then leave to live.

[1] Licensed for the stage, May 27, 1624.

From JOHN FLETCHER'S *The Nice Valour, or the Passionate Madman*, 1647.[1]

SHOOT MORE, SHOOT MORE!

THOU deity, swift-winged Love,
   Sometimes below, sometimes above,
Little in shape, but great in power;
Thou that makest a heart thy tower,
And thy loopholes ladies' eyes,
From whence thou strikest the fond and wise;
Did all the shafts in thy fair quiver
Stick fast in my ambitious liver,
Yet thy power would I adore,
And call upon thee to shoot more,
   Shoot more, shoot more!

FAIR CUPID, TURN AWAY THY BOW!

OH, turn thy bow!
   Thy power we feel and know;
Fair Cupid, turn away thy bow!
They be those golden arrows,
Bring ladies all their sorrows;
   And till there be more truth in men,
   Never shoot at maid again!

---

[1] The date of the play is uncertain; nor can the dates of the three following plays be fixed with accuracy.

NOUGHT SO SWEET AS MELANCHOLY.

HENCE, all you vain delights,
As short as are the nights
Wherein you spend your folly!
There's nought in this life sweet,
If man were wise to see't,
But only melancholy,
Oh, sweetest melancholy!
Welcome, folded arms, and fixed eyes,
A sight that piercing mortifies,
A look that's fastened to the ground,
A tongue chained up without a sound!

Fountain-heads, and pathless groves,
Places which pale passion loves!
Moonlight walks, when all the fowls
Are warmly housed, save bats and owls!
A midnight bell, a parting groan!
These are the sounds we feed upon;
Then stretch our bones in a still gloomy valley,
Nothing's so dainty sweet as lovely melancholy.

BRAVE ANGER!

A CURSE upon thee, for a slave!
Art thou here, and heard'st me rave?
Fly not sparkles from mine eye,
To show my indignation nigh?
Am I not all foam and fire,
With voice as hoarse as a town-crier?
How my back opes and shuts together
With fury, as old men's with weather!
Could'st thou not hear my teeth gnash hither?
Death, hell, fiends, and darkness!
I will thrash thy mangy carcase!
There cannot be too many tortures
Spent upon those lousy quarters.
Thou nasty, scurvy, mongrel toad,
    Mischief on thee!
    Light upon thee .
All the plagues that can confound thee,
Or did ever reign abroad!
Better a thousand lives it cost,
Than have brave anger spilt or lost.

HA, HA, HA!

OH, how my lungs do tickle! ha, ha, ha!
   Oh, how my lungs do tickle! ho, ho, ho, ho!
     Set a sharp jest
     Against my breast,
Then how my lungs do tickle!
     As nightingales,
     And things in cambric rails,[1]
Sing best against a prickle.
     Ha, ha, ha, ha!
     Ho, ho, ho, ho, ho!
Laugh! Laugh! Laugh! Laugh!
Wide! Loud! And vary!
A smile is for a simpering novice,
    One that ne'er tasted caviare,
Nor knows the smack of dear anchovies.
     Ha, ha, ha, ha, ha!
     Ho, ho, ho, ho, ho!
A giggling waiting wench for me,
That shows her teeth how white they be!
A thing not fit for gravity,
For theirs are foul and hardly three.
     Ha, ha, ha!
     Ho, ho, ho!
Democritus, thou ancient fleerer.
   How I miss thy laugh, and ha' since!
There you named the famous['t] jeerer,
   That ever jeered in Rome or Athens.
     Ha, ha, ha!
     Ho, ho, ho!

---

[1] Night-rails (night-dresses).

How brave lives he that keeps a fool,
    Although the rate be deeper!
But he that is his own fool, sir,
    Does live a great deal cheaper.
Sure I shall burst, burst, quite break,
    Thou art so witty.
'Tis rare to break at court,
    For that belongs to the city.
Ha, ha! my spleen is almost worn
    To the last laughter.
Oh, keep a corner for a friend;
    A jest may come hereafter.

From JOHN FLETCHER'S *Love's Cure*, 1647.

TURN, TURN THY BEAUTEOUS FACE AWAY.

TURN, turn thy beauteous face away;
    How pale and sickly looks the day,
In emulation of thy brighter beams!
Oh envious light, fly, fly, begone!
Come, night, and piece two breasts as one!
When what love does we will repeat in dreams.
Yet, thy eyes open, who can day hence fright?
Let but their lids fall, and it will be night.

From JOHN FLETCHER'S *The Queen of Corinth*, 1647.

WEEP NO MORE.

WEEP no more, nor sigh, nor groan,
Sorrow calls no time that's gone:
Violets plucked, the sweetest rain
Makes not fresh nor grow again;
Trim thy locks, look cheerfully;
Fate's hid ends eyes cannot see:
Joys as winged dreams fly fast,
Why should sadness longer last?
Grief is but a wound to woe;
Gentlest fair, mourn, mourn no mo.[1]

From JOHN FLETCHER'S *The Bloody Brother; or, Rollo, Duke of Normandy*, 1639.

DRINK TO-DAY, AND DROWN ALL SORROW.

DRINK to-day, and drown all sorrow,
You shall perhaps not do it to-morrow:
Best, while you have it, use your breath;
There is no drinking after death.

Wine works the heart up, wakes the wit,
There is no cure 'gainst age but it:
It helps the head-ache, cough, and tisic,
And is for all diseases physic.

Then let us swill, boys, for our health;
Who drinks well, loves the commonwealth.
And he that will to bed go sober
Falls with the leaf still in October.

[1] " No mo "—no more.

From John Fletcher's *The Elder Brother*, 1637.

BEAUTY CLEAR AND FAIR.

Beauty clear and fair,
    Where the air
Rather like a perfume dwells;
  Where the violet and the rose
  Their blue veins and[1] blush disclose,
And come to honour nothing else.

Where to live near,
    And planted there,
Is to live, and still live new;
  Where to gain a favour is
  More than light, perpetual bliss,—
Make me live by serving you.

Dear, again back recall
    To this light,
A stranger to himself and all;
  Both the wonder and the story
  Shall be yours, and eke the glory:
I am your servant, and your thrall.

---

[1] Old eds. "in"—which Dyce retained. Mason proposed "and"; and this reading is found in an early MS. copy of the play (Egerton MS. 1994).

From FLETCHER and ROWLEY'S
The Maid in the Mill, 1647.[1]

COME FOLLOW ME, YOU COUNTRY LASSES.

COME follow me, you country lasses,
And you shall see such sport as passes:
You shall dance and I will sing;
Pedro, he shall rub the string;
Each shall have a loose-bodied gown
Of green, and laugh till you lie down.
  Come follow me, come follow, &c.

You shall have crowns of roses, daisies,
Buds where the honey-maker grazes;
You shall taste the golden thighs,
Such as in wax-chamber lies:
What fruit please you taste, freely pull,
Till you have all your bellies full.
  Come follow me, &c.

[1] Acted in 1623.—I suspect that the song may be by William Rowley.

From SHAKESPEARE and FLETCHER'S *The Two Noble Kinsmen*, 1634.

A BRIDAL SONG.[1]

ROSES, their sharp spines being gone,
Not royal in their smells alone,
   But in their hue;
Maiden pinks, of odour faint,
Daisies smell-less, yet most quaint,
   And sweet thyme true;

Primrose, firstborn child of Ver,
Merry springtime's harbinger,
   With her bells dim;[2]
Oxlips in their cradles growing,
Marigolds on deathbeds blowing,
   Larks'-heels trim.

All dear Nature's children sweet,
Lie 'fore bride and bridegroom's feet,
   Blessing their sense!
Not an angel of the air,
Bird melodious, or bird fair,
   Be absent hence!

The crow, the slanderous cuckoo, nor
The boding raven, nor chough hoar,[3]
   Nor chattering pie,
May on our bride-house perch or sing,
Or with them any discord bring,
   But from it fly!

---

[1] I have given the song tentatively to Fletcher; but I have a strong suspicion that it is by Shakespeare.

[2] Mr. W. J. Linton proposes "With harebell slim."

[3] "Chough hoar" is Seward's correction. Old eds. "clough hee" (and "he").

URNS AND ODOURS BRING AWAY!

URNS and odours bring away!
 Vapours, sighs, darken the day!
Our dole[1] more deadly looks than dying;
 Balms, and gums, and heavy cheers,
 Sacred vials filled with tears,
And clamours through the wild air flying!

Come, all sad and solemn shows,
That are quick-eyed Pleasure's foes!
We convent nought else but woes.

From *King Henry VIII.*, 1623.

THE POWER OF MUSIC.

ORPHEUS with his lute made trees,
 And the mountain-tops that freeze,
 Bow themselves when he did sing:
To his music plants and flowers
Ever sprung; as sun and showers
 There had made a lasting spring.

Everything that heard him play,.
Even the billows of the sea,
 Hung their heads, and then lay by.
In sweet music is such art,
Killing care and grief of heart
 Fall asleep, or, hearing, die.

[1] Sorrow.

> From JOHN WEBSTER'S *The White Devil*, 1612.

A DIRGE.

CALL for the robin-redbreast and the wren,
  Since o'er shady groves they hover,
And with leaves and flowers do cover
The friendless bodies of unburied men.
Call unto his funeral dole
The ant, the field-mouse, and the mole,
To rear him hillocks that shall keep him warm,
And (when gay tombs are robbed) sustain no harm ;
But keep the wolf far thence, that's foe to men,
For with his nails he'll dig them up again.

> From JOHN WEBSTER'S *The Duchess of Malfi*, 1623.

HARK, NOW EVERYTHING IS STILL.

HARK, now everything is still,
  The screech-owl and the whistler shrill,
Call upon our dame aloud,
And bid her quickly don her shroud !
Much you had of land and rent ;
Your length in clay's now competent :
A long war disturbed your mind ;
Here your perfect peace is signed.
Of what is't fools make such vain keeping ?
Sin their conception, their birth weeping,

Their life a general mist of error,
Their death a hideous storm of terror.
Strew your hair with powders sweet,
Don clean linen, bathe your feet,
And (the foul fiend more to check)
A crucifix let bless your neck :
'Tis now full tide 'tween night and day ;
End your groan, and come away.

From JOHN WEBSTER'S *The Devil's Law-Case*, 1623.

VANITAS VANITATUM.

ALL the flowers of the spring
Meet to perfume our burying ;
These have but their growing prime,
And man does flourish but his time :
Survey our progress from our birth ;
We are set, we grow, we turn to earth.
Courts adieu, and all delights,
All bewitching appetites !
Sweetest breath and clearest eye,
Like perfumes, go out and die ;
And consequently this is done
As shadows wait upon the sun.
Vain the ambition of kings
Who seek by trophies and dead things
To leave a living name behind,
And weave but nets to catch the wind.

From JOHN FORD'S *The Lover's Melancholy*, 1629.

FLY HENCE, SHADOWS!

FLY hence, shadows, that do keep
  Watchful sorrows charmed in sleep!
Tho' the eyes be overtaken,
Yet the heart doth ever waken
Thoughts, chained up in busy snares
Of continual woes and cares:
Love and griefs are so exprest
As they rather sigh than rest.
Fly hence, shadows, that do keep
Watchful sorrows charmed in sleep!

From JOHN FORD'S *The Broken Heart*, 1633.

A BRIDAL SONG.

COMFORTS lasting, loves increasing,
  Like soft hours never ceasing;
Plenty's pleasure, peace complying,
Without jars, or tongues envying;
Hearts by holy union wedded,
More than theirs by custom bedded;
Fruitful issues; life so graced,
Not by age to be defaced;
Budding as the year ensu'th,
Every spring another youth:
All what thought can add beside,
Crown this Bridegroom and this Bride!

From THOMAS HEYWOOD'S *Fair
Maid of the Exchange*, 1607.

YE LITTLE BIRDS THAT SIT AND SING.

YE little birds that sit and sing
   Amidst the shady valleys,
And see how Phillis sweetly walks
   Within her garden-alleys ;
Go, pretty birds, about her bower ;
Sing, pretty birds, she may not lower ;
Ah, me ! methinks I see her frown !
   Ye pretty wantons, warble.

Go, tell her through your chirping bills,
   As you by me are bidden,
To her is only known my love,
   Which from the world is hidden.
Go, pretty birds, and tell her so ;
See that your notes strain not too low,
For still, methinks, I see her frown ;
   Ye pretty wantons, warble.

Go, tune your voices' harmony,
   And sing, I am her lover ;
Strain loud and sweet, that every note
   With sweet content may move her :
And she that hath the sweetest voice,
Tell her I will not change my choice ;
Yet still, methinks, I see her frown !
   Ye pretty wantons, warble.

Oh, fly! make haste! see, see, she falls
   Into a pretty slumber.
Sing round about her rosy bed,
   That waking, she may wonder.
Say to her, 'tis her lover true
That sendeth love to you, to you;
And when you hear her kind reply,
   Return with pleasant warblings.

From THOMAS HEYWOOD'S *The Rape of Lucrece*, 1608.

PACK, CLOUDS, AWAY!

PACK, clouds, away, and welcome, day!
   With night we banish sorrow.
Sweet air, blow soft; mount, lark, aloft
To give my love good morrow.
Wings from the wind to please her mind,
Notes from the lark I'll borrow:
Bird, prune thy wing, nightingale, sing,
To give my love good morrow.
To give my love good morrow,
Notes from them all I'll borrow.

Wake from thy nest, robin redbreast!
Sing, birds, in every furrow,
And from each bill let music shrill
Give my fair love good morrow.
Black-bird and thrush in every bush,
'Stare,'[1] linnet, and cock-sparrow,
You pretty elves, amongst yourselves
Sing my fair love good morrow.
To give my love good morrow,
Sing, birds, in every furrow.

[1] Starling.

From THOMAS HEYWOOD'S *Golden Age*, 1611.

DIAN'S VOTARIES.

HAIL, beauteous Dian, queen of shades,
That dwells beneath these shadowy glades,
Mistress of all those beauteous maids
   That are by her allowed.
Virginity we all profess,
Abjure the worldly vain excess,
And will to Dian yield no less
   Than we to her have vowed.
The shepherds, satyrs, nymphs, and fauns,
For thee will trip it o'er the lawns.

Come, to the forest let us go,
And trip it like the barren doe;
The fauns and satyrs still do so,
   And freely thus they may do.
The fairies dance and satyrs sing,
And on the grass tread many a ring,
And to their caves their venison bring;
   And we will do as they do.
      The shepherds, satyrs, &c., &c.

Our food is honey from the bees,
And mellow fruits that drop from trees;
In chase we climb the high degrees
   Of every steepy mountain.
And when the weary day is past,
We at the evening hie us fast,
And after this, our field repast,
   We drink the pleasant fountain.
      The shepherds, satyrs, &c., &c.

From Thomas Heywood's *Silver Age*, 1613.

PRAISE OF CERES.

WITH fair Ceres, Queen of Grain,
  The reaped fields we roam, roam, roam:
Each country peasant, nymph, and swain,
  Sing their harvest home, home, home;
Whilst the Queen of Plenty hallows
Growing fields as well as fallows.

Echo, double all our lays,
  Make the champians[1] sound, sound, sound,
To the Queen of Harvest's praise,
  That sows and reaps our ground, ground, ground.
Ceres, Queen of Plenty, hallows
Growing fields as well as fallows.

From Thomas Heywood's *A Maidenhead well lost*, 1634.

LOVE'S ECSTASY.

HENCE with passion, sighs, and tears,
  Disasters, sorrows, cares and fears!
See, my Love, my Love, appears,
  That thought himself exiled.
Whence might all these loud joys grow,
Whence might mirth and banquets flow,
But that he's come, he's come, I know?
  Fair Fortune, thou hast smiled.

[1] An old form of "champaigns."

Give [un]to these windows eyes,
Daze the stars and mock the skies,
And let us two, us two, devise
    To lavish our best treasures :
Crown our wishes with content,
Meet our souls in sweet consent,
And let this night, this night, be spent
    In all abundant pleasures.

From THOMAS HEYWOOD'S *Love's Mistress*, 1636.

TO PHŒBUS.

PHŒBUS, unto thee we sing,
  O thou great Idalian king ;
Thou the God of Physic art,
Of Poetry and Archery :
We sing unto thee with a heart
Devoted to thy deity.
All bright glory crown thy head,
Thou sovereign of all piety,
Whose golden beams and rays are shed
As well upon the poor as rich,
For thou alike regardest each.
Phœbus, unto thee we sing,
O thou great Idalian king.

From THOMAS HEYWOOD'S
Pleasant Dialogues, 1637.

SEMEL IN ANNO RIDET APOLLO.

HOWSOE'ER the minutes go,
Run the hours or swift or slow,
Seem the months or short or long,
Pass the seasons right or wrong,
All we sing, that Phœbus follow,
" Semel in anno ridet Apollo."

Early fall the spring or not,
Prove the summer cold or hot,
Autumn be it fair or foul,
Let the winter smile or scowl,
Still we sing, that Phœbus follow,
" Semel in anno ridet Apollo."

RUSTIC HAPPINESS.

WE that have known no greater state
Than this we live in, praise our fate;
For courtly silks in cares are spent
When country's russet breeds content.
The power of sceptres we admire,
But sheep-hooks for our use desire.
Simple and low is our condition,
For here with us is no ambition.
We with the sun our flocks unfold,
Whose rising makes their fleeces gold:
Our music from the birds we borrow,
They bidding us, we them, good morrow.

Our habits are but coarse and plain,
Yet they defend from wind and rain,
As warm too in an equal eye
As those be, stained in scarlet dye :
Those that have plenty wear, we see,
But one at once, and so do we.
The shepherd with his home-spun lass
As many merry hours doth pass
As courtiers with their costly girls,
Though richly decked in gold and pearls.

From WILLIAM ROWLEY'S *The Thracian Wonder*,[1] 1661.

AGAINST LOVE.

LOVE is a law, a discord of such force,
That 'twixt our sense and reason makes divorce ;
Love's a desire, that to obtain betime,
We lose an age of years plucked from our prime ;
Love is a thing to which we soon consent,
As soon refuse, but sooner far repent.

Then what must women be, that are the cause
That love hath life? that lovers feel such laws?
They're like the winds upon Lepanthæ's shore,
That still are changing : O, then love no more !
A woman's love is like that Syrian flower
That buds and spreads and withers in an hour.

[1] Francis Kirkman published this play in 1661 and attributed it on the title-page to Webster and William Rowley. Webster had certainly no hand in it.—The date of composition cannot be fixed.

DELAY IN LOVE'S A LINGERING PAIN.

I CARE not for these idle toys
   That must be wooed and prayed to;
Come, sweet love, let's use the joys
   That men and women use to do.

The first man had a woman
   Created for his use, you know;
Then never seek so close to keep
   A jewel of a price so low.

Delay in love's a lingering pain
   That never can be cured;
Unless that love have love again,
   'Tis not to be endured.

HOLLA, HOLLA!

ART thou gone in haste?
   I'll not forsake thee;
Runn'st thou ne'er so fast,
   I'll o'ertake thee:
O'er the dales, o'er the downs,
   Through the green meadows,
From the fields through the towns,
   To the dim shadows.

All along the plain,
  To the low fountains,
Up and down again
  From the high mountains;
Echo then shall again
  Tell her I follow,
And the floods to the woods,
  Carry my holla, holla!
  Ce! la! ho! ho! hu!

OLD FATHER JANEVERE.

NOW[1] does jolly Janus greet your merriment;
  For since the world's creation,
I never changed my fashion;
'Tis good enough to fence the cold:
My hatchet serves to cut my firing yearly,
My bowl preserves the juice of grape and barley:
Fire, wine, and strong beer, make me live so long here
To give the merry New-year a welcome in.

All the potent powers of plenty wait upon
You that intend to be frolic to-day:
To Bacchus I commend ye, and Ceres eke attend ye,
To keep encroaching cares away.
That Boreas' blasts may never blow to harm you;
Nor Hyems' frosts but give you cause to warm you:
Old father Janevere drinks a health to all here,
To give the merry New-year a welcome in.

[1] The stage-direction is "*Enter* Titterus *like old* Janus, *with a coat girt to him, a white Beard and Hair; a Hatchet in one hand, and a Bowl in the other, he sings.*"

DEPARTURE OF JANEVERE.

SINCE you desire my absence;
   I will depart this green;
Though loath to leave the presence
   Of such a lovely queen;
Whose beauty, like the sun,
   Melts all my frost away;
And now, instead of Winter,
   Behold a youthful May.

LOVE'S A LOVELY LAD.

LOVE'S a lovely lad,
   His bringing-up is beauty;
Who loves him not is mad,
   For I must pay him duty;
     Now I'm sad.

Hail to those sweet eyes,
   That shine celestial wonder!
From thence do flames arise,
   Burn my poor heart asunder.
     Now it fries.

Cupid sets a crown
   Upon those lovely tresses;
O, spoil not with a frown
   What he so sweetly dresses!
     I'll sit down.

WHITHER SHALL I GO?

WHITHER shall I go,
  To escape away from folly?
For now there's love I know,
  Or else 'tis melancholy:
    Heigh, heigho!

Yonder lies the snow,
  But my heart cannot melt it:
Love shoots from his bow,
  And my poor heart hath felt it.
    Heigh, heigho!

I'LL NE'ER LOVE MORE.

O STAY, O turn, O pity me
  That sighs, that sues for love of thee!
O lack! I never loved before;
If you deny, I'll ne'er love more.

No hope, no help! then wretched I
Must lose, must lack, must pine, and die;
Since you neglect when I implore.
Farewell, hard, I'll ne'er love more.

MEN, BEWARE.

THERE is not any wise man,
  That fancy can a woman ;
Then never turn your eyes on
A thing that is so common :
For be they foul or fair,
They tempting devils are,
Since they first fell ;
They that love do live in hell,
And therefore, men, beware.

O, THE DEVIL TAKE YOU ALL !

FOOLISH, idle toys,
  That nature gave unto us,
But to curb our joys,
And only to undo us ;
For since Lucretia's fall,
There are none chaste at all ;
Or if perchance there be
One in an empery,
Some other malady
Makes her far worse than she.
    Out upon ye all !

'Twere too much to tell
The follies that attend ye ;
He must love you well
That can but discommend ye ;
For your deserts are such,
Man cannot rail too much ;
Nor is the world so blind,
But it may easily find
The body, or [the] mind,
Tainted in womankind.
  O, the devil take you all !

TO APOLLO.

FAIR Apollo, whose bright beams
 Cheers all the world below :
The birds that sing, the plants that spring,
The herbs and flowers that grow :
O, lend thy aid to a swain sore oppressed,
  That his mind
  Soon may find
The delight that sense admits !
And by a maid let his harms be redressed,
  That no pain
  Do remain
In his mind to offend his wits !

> From THOMAS MIDDLETON and
> WILLIAM ROWLEY'S *The
> World tost at Tennis*, 1620.

SIMPLICITY.

HAPPY times we live to see,
  Whose master is Simplicity:
This is the age where blessings flow,
In joy we reap, in peace we sow;
We do good deeds without delay,
We promise and we keep our day;
We love for virtue, not for wealth,
We drink no healths but all for health;
We sing, we dance, we pipe, we play,
Our work's continual holiday;
We live in poor contented sort,
Yet neither beg nor come at court.

> From THOMAS MIDDLETON and
> WILLIAM ROWLEY'S *The
> Spanish Gipsy*, 1653.[1]

TRIP IT, GIPSIES.

TRIP it, gipsies, trip it fine,
  Show tricks and lofty capers;
At threading-needles[2] we repine,
  And leaping over rapiers:
Pindy-pandy rascal toys!
  We scorn cutting purses;
Though we live by making noise,
  For cheating none can curse us.

---

[1] Written not later than 1623.   [2] An old pastime.

Over high ways, over low,
    And over stones and gravel,
Though we trip it on the toe,
    And thus for silver travel;
Though our dances waste our backs,
    At night fat capons mend them;
Eggs well brewed in buttered sack,
    Our wenches say befriend them.

Oh that all the world were mad!
    Then should we have fine dancing;
Hobby-horses would be had,
    And brave girls keep a-prancing;
Beggars would on cock-horse ride,
    And boobies fall a-roaring;
And cuckolds, though no horns be spied,
    Be one another goring.

Welcome, poet to our ging![1]
    Make rhymes, we'll give thee reason,
Canary bees thy brains shall sting,
    Mull-sack did ne'er speak treason;
Peter-see-me[2] shall wash thy nowl,[3]
    And Malaga glasses fox[4] thee;
If, poet, thou toss not bowl for bowl,
    Thou shalt not kiss a doxy.

[1] Company.
[2] A corruption of *Pedro Ximenes*, a delicate Spanish wine.
[3] Noddle.   [4] Intoxicate.

SA, SA, THE GIPSIES' ARMY COMES.

  COME, follow your leader, follow;
   Our convoy be Mars and Apollo!
  The van comes brave up here;
Answer. As hotly comes the rear.
Chorus.   Our knackers are the fifes and drums,
    Sa, sa, the gipsies' army comes!

  Horsemen we need not fear,
  There's none but footmen here;
  The horse sure charge without;
  Or if they wheel about,
Chorus.   Our knackers are the shot that fly,
    Pit-a-pat rattling in the sky.

  If once the great ordnance play,
  That's laughing, yet run not away,
  But stand the push of pike,
  Scorn can but basely strike;
Chorus.   Then let our armies join and sing,
    And pit-a-pat make our knackers ring.

  Arm, arm! what bands are those?
  They cannot be sure our foes;
  We'll not draw up our force,
  Nor muster any horse;
Chorus.   For since they pleased to view our sight,
    Let's this way, this way, give delight.

>   A council of war let's call,
>   Look either to stand or fall;
>   If our weak army stands,
>   Thank all these noble hands;
>
> *Chorus.*   Whose gates of love being open thrown,
>   We enter, and then the town's our own.

GIPSY RITES.

THY best hand lay on this turf of grass,
There thy heart lies, vow not to pass
From us two years for sun nor snow,
For hill nor dale, howe'er winds blow;
Vow the hard earth to be thy bed,
With her green cushions under thy head;
Flower-banks or moss to be thy board,
Water thy wine—and drink like a lord.
    Kings can have but coronations;
    We are as proud of gipsy fashions;
    Dance, sing, and in a well-mixed border,
    Close this new brother of our order.

What we get with us come share,
You to get must vow to care;
Nor strike gipsy, nor stand by
When strangers strike, but fight or die;
Our gipsy-wenches are not common,
You must not kiss a fellow's leman;
Nor to your own, for one you must,
In songs send errands of base lust.
    Dance, sing, and in a well-mixed border
    Close this new brother of our order.

* * * * * *

Set foot to foot; those garlands hold,
Now mark [well] what more is told;
By cross arms, the lover's sign,
Vow as these flowers themselves entwine,
Of April's wealth building a throne
Round, so your love to one or none;
By those touches of your feet,
You must each night embracing meet,
Chaste, howe'er disjoined by day;
You the sun with her must play,
She to you the marigold,
To none but you her leaves unfold;
Wake she or sleep, your eyes so charm,
Want, woe, nor weather do her harm.
This is your market now of kisses,
Buy and sell free each other blisses.
    Holidays, high days, gipsy-fairs,
    When kisses are fairings, and hearts meet in
        pairs.

From THOMAS MIDDLETON'S
Blurt, Master Constable, 1602.

LIPS AND EYES.

LOVE for such a cherry lip
   Would be glad to pawn his arrows;
Venus here to take a sip
   Would sell her doves and teams of sparrows.
     But they shall not so;
       Hey nonny, nonny no!
    None but I this lip must owe,[1]
       Hey nonny, nonny no!

[1] Old form of "own."

Did Jove see this wanton eye,
  Ganymede must wait no longer;
Phœbe[1] here one night did lie,
  Would change her face and look much younger.
    But they shall not so;
      Hey nonny, nonny no!
    None but I this lip must owe;
      Hey nonny, nonny no!

From Thomas Middleton's *A Mad World, my Masters*, 1608.

O FOR A BOWL OF FAT CANARY.

O FOR a bowl of fat canary,
  Rich Aristippus, sparkling sherry!
Some nectar else from Juno's dairy;
O these draughts would make us merry!

O for a wench! I deal in faces,
And in other daintier things;
Tickled am I with her embraces;
Fine dancing in such fairy rings!

O for a plump, fat leg of mutton,
Veal, lamb, capon, pig, and coney!
None is happy but a glutton,
None an ass, but who wants money.

Wines, indeed, and girls are good;
But brave victuals feast the blood;
For wenches, wine, and lusty cheer,
Jove would come down to surfeit here.

---

[1] *i.e.* "did Phœbe here," &c.

From Thomas Middleton's *A Chaste Maid in Cheapside*,[1] 1630.

MY LOVE AND I MUST PART.

WEEP eyes, break heart!
  My love and I must part.
Cruel fates true love do soonest sever;
O, I shall see thee never, never, never!
O, happy is the maid whose life takes end
Ere it knows parent's frown or loss of friend!
Weep eyes, break heart!
My love and I must part.

From Thomas Middleton's *The Witch*, 16..?

MAID, WIFE, AND WIDOW.

IN a maiden-time professed,
  Then we say that life is blessed;
Tasting once the married life,
Then we only praise the wife;
There's but one state more to try,
Which makes women laugh or cry—
Widow, widow: of these three
The middle's best, and that give me.

---

[1] Produced circ. 1613.

HECATE AND THE WITCHES.

Voices above. COME away, come away,
Hecate, Hecate, come away.
Hecate. I come, I come, I come, I come,
With all the speed I may,
With all the speed I may.
Where's Stadlin?
Voice above. Here.
Hecate. Where's Puckle?
Voice above. Here,
And Hoppo too, and Hellwain too;
We lack but you, we lack but you;
Come away, make up the count.
Hecate. I will but 'noint, and then I mount.
[*A spirit like a cat descends.*
Voice above. There's one comes down to fetch his dues,
A kiss, a coll, a sip of blood;
And why thou stayest so long
I muse, I muse,
Since the air's so sweet and good.
Hecate. O, art thou come?
What news, what news?
Spirit. All goes still to our delight:
Either come, or else
Refuse, refuse.
Hecate. Now I'm furnished for the flight.
Now I go, now I fly,
Malkin my sweet spirit and I.
O what a dainty pleasure 'tis

To ride in the air
When the moon shines fair,
And sing and dance, and toy and kiss!
Over woods, high rocks, and mountains,
Over seas, our mistress' fountains,
Over steeples, towers, and turrets,
We fly by night, 'mongst troops of spirits:
No ring of bells to our ears sounds,
No howls of wolves, no yelps of hounds;
No, not the noise of water's breach,
Or cannon's throat our height can reach.

A CHARM-SONG.

Black spirits and white, red spirits and gray,
Mingle, mingle, mingle, you that mingle may!
    Titty, Tiffin,
    Keep it stiff in;
    Firedrake, Puckey,
    Make it lucky;
    Liard, Robin,
    You must bob in.
Round, around, around, about, about!
All ill come running in, all good keep out!

1 *Witch.* Here's the blood of a bat.
Hecate. Put in that, O put in that!
2 *Witch.* Here's libbard's bane.
Hecate. Put in again!

1 *Witch.* The juice of toad, the oil of adder;
2 *Witch.* Those will make the younker madder.
Hecate. Put in—there's all—and rid the stench.
Firestone. Nay, here's three ounces of the red-haired wench.
All. Round, around, around, about, about!

From *The Widow*, 1652.[1]

THE THIEVES' SONG.

HOW round the world goes, and every thing that's in it!
The tides of gold and silver ebb and flow in a minute:
From the usurer to his sons, there a current swiftly runs;
From the sons to queans in chief, from the gallant to the thief;
From the thief unto his host, from the host to husbandmen;
From the country to the court; and so it comes to us again.
How round the world goes, and every thing that's in it!
The tides of gold and silver ebb and flow in a minute.

[1] Ascribed to Jonson, Fletcher, and Middleton. Written circ. 1616.

From THOMAS MIDDLETON'S
More Dissemblers besides Women, 1657.[1]

THE GIPSIES.

Gipsy Captain. COME, my dainty doxies,
  My dells,[2] my dells most dear;
 We have neither house nor land,
  Yet never want good cheer.
Chorus. We never want good cheer.
Gipsy Captain. We take no care for candle rents,
2 Gipsy. We lie.   *3 Gipsy.* We snort.
Gipsy Captain. We sport in tents,
 Then rouse betimes and steal our
  Our store is never taken [dinners.
  Without pigs, hens, or bacon,
 And that's good meat for sinners:
  At wakes and fairs we cozen
  Poor country folks by dozen;
 If one have money, he disburses;
 Whilst some tell fortunes, some pick
  Rather than be out of use, [purses;
  We'll steal garters, hose or shoes,
 Boots, or spurs with gingling rowels,
 Shirts or napkins, smocks or towels.
  Come live with us, come live with us,
  All you that love your eases;
   He that's a gipsy
   May be drunk or tipsy
  At any hour he pleases.
Chorus. We laugh, we quaff, we roar, we scuffle;
 We cheat, we drab, we filch, we shuffle.

---

[1] Written not later than 1623.   [2] Cant term for "maids."

From *The Mountebank's Masque*,
performed February, 1617-8.

THE DAY MUST HAVE HER NIGHT, THE SPRING HER FALL.

THE hour of sweety night decays apace,
And now warm beds are better than this place.
—All time is long that is unwilling spent,
But hours are minutes when they yield content.—
The gathered flowers we love that breathe sweet scent,
But loathe them, their sweet odours being spent.—
    It is a life is never ill
    To lie and sleep in roses still.—

The rarer pleasure is it is more sweet,
And friends are kindest when they seldom meet.—
Who would not hear the nightingale still sing,
Or who grew ever weary of the spring?—
The day must have her night, the spring her fall,
All is divided, none is lord of all.—
    It were a most delightful thing
    To live in a perpetual spring.

From *Histriomastix*, 1610.

THE NUT-BROWN ALE.

THE nut-brown ale, the nut-brown ale,
Puts down all drink when it is stale!
The toast, the nutmeg, and the ginger
Will make a sighing man a singer.
Ale gives a buffet in the head,
  But ginger under-props the brain;
When ale would strike a strong man dead
  Then nutmeg tempers it again.
The nut-brown ale, the nut-brown ale,
Puts down all drink when it is stale!

From WILLIAM BROWNE'S *The Inner Temple Masque*, 1614-5.

SONG OF THE SIRENS.

STEER hither, steer your winged pines,
    All-beaten mariners !
Here lie Love's undiscovered mines,
    A prey to passengers ;
Perfumes far sweeter than the best
Which make the Phœnix' urn and nest.
    Fear not your ships,
Nor any to oppose you save our lips ;
    But come on shore
Where no joy dies till love hath gotten more.

For swelling waves our panting breasts,
    Where never storms arise,
Exchange, and be awhile our guests ;
    For stars gaze on our eyes.
The compass love shall hourly sing,
And as he goes about the ring,
    We will not miss
To tell each point he nameth with a kiss.

Chorus.
Then come on shore,
Where no joy dies till love hath gotten more.

From PHINEAS FLETCHER'S *Sicelides*, 1614.

LOVE.

LOVE is the sire, dam, nurse, and seed
Of all that air, earth, waters breed :
All these, earth, water, air, fire,
Though contraries, in love conspire.
Fond painters, love is not a lad
With bow, and shafts, and feathers clad,
As he is fancied in the brain
Of some loose loving idle swain.
Much sooner is he felt than seen ;
His substance subtle, slight and thin.
Oft leaps he from the glancing eyes ;
Oft in some smooth mount he lies ;
Soonest he wins, the fastest flies ;
Oft lurks he 'twixt the ruddy lips,
Thence, while the heart his nectar sips,
Down to the soul the poison slips ;
Oft in a voice creeps down the ear ;
Oft hides his darts in golden hair ;
Oft blushing cheeks do light his fires ;
Oft in a smooth soft skin retires ;
Often in smiles, often in tears,
His flaming heat in water bears ;
When nothing else kindles desire,
Even virtue's self shall blow the fire.
Love with thousand darts abounds,
Surest and deepest virtue wounds ;
Oft himself becomes a dart,
And love with love doth love impart.
Thou painful pleasure, pleasing pain,
Thou gainful loss,[1] thou losing gain,

[1] Old ed. "life."

From WILLIAM BROWNE'S *The Inner Temple Masque*, 1614-5.

SONG OF THE SIRENS.

STEER hither, steer your winged pines,
 All-beaten mariners!
Here lie Love's undiscovered mines,
 A prey to passengers;
Perfumes far sweeter than the best
Which make the Phœnix' urn and nest.
  Fear not your ships,
Nor any to oppose you save our lips;
  But come on shore
Where no joy dies till love hath gotten more.

For swelling waves our panting breasts,
 Where never storms arise,
Exchange, and be awhile our guests;
 For stars gaze on our eyes.
The compass love shall hourly sing,
And as he goes about the ring,
  We will not miss
To tell each point he nameth with a kiss.

Chorus.
Then come on shore,
Where no joy dies till love hath gotten more.

From PHINEAS FLETCHER'S *Sicel-ides*, 1614.

LOVE.

LOVE is the sire, dam, nurse, and seed
Of all that air, earth, waters breed:
All these, earth, water, air, fire,
Though contraries, in love conspire.
Fond painters, love is not a lad
With bow, and shafts, and feathers clad,
As he is fancied in the brain
Of some loose loving idle swain.
Much sooner is he felt than seen;
His substance subtle, slight and thin.
Oft leaps he from the glancing eyes;
Oft in some smooth mount he lies;
Soonest he wins, the fastest flies;
Oft lurks he 'twixt the ruddy lips,
Thence, while the heart his nectar sips,
Down to the soul the poison slips;
Oft in a voice creeps down the ear;
Oft hides his darts in golden hair;
Oft blushing cheeks do light his fires;
Oft in a smooth soft skin retires;
Often in smiles, often in tears,
His flaming heat in water bears;
When nothing else kindles desire,
Even virtue's self shall blow the fire.
Love with thousand darts abounds,
Surest and deepest virtue wounds;
Oft himself becomes a dart,
And love with love doth love impart.
Thou painful pleasure, pleasing pain,
Thou gainful loss,[1] thou losing gain,

[1] Old ed. "life."

Thou bitter sweet, easing disease,
How dost thou by displeasing please?
How dost thou thus bewitch the heart,
To love in hate, to joy in smart,
To think itself most bound when free,
And freest in its slavery?
Every creature is thy debtor;
None but loves, some worse, some better.
Only in love they happy prove
Who love what most deserves their love.

From SAMUEL ROWLEY'S [?] *The Noble Spanish Soldier*, 1634.

OH, SORROW, SORROW.

OH, sorrow, sorrow, say where dost thou dwell?
   In the lowest room of hell.
Art thou born of human race?
   No, no, I have a fury's [1] face.
Art thou in city, town, or court?
   I to every place resort.
Oh, why into the world is sorrow sent?
   Men afflicted best repent.
What dost thou feed on?
   Broken sleep.
What takest thou pleasure in?
   To weep,
   To sigh, to sob, to pine, to groan,
   To wring my hands, to sit alone.
Oh when, oh when shall sorrow quiet have?
   Never, never, never, never.
   Never till she finds a grave.

[1] Old ed. "furier."

From NATHANIEL FIELD'S *A Woman is a Weathercock*, 1612.

PARI JUGO DULCIS TRACTUS.

THEY that for worldly wealth do wed,
That buy and sell the marriage-bed,
That come not warmed with the true fire,
Resolved to keep this vow entire,
    Too soon find discontent :
    Too soon shall they repent.
But, Hymen, these are no such lovers,
Which thy burning torch discovers :
Though they live, then, many a year,
Let each day as new appear
    As this first ; and delights
    Make of all bridal nights.
Io, Hymen ! give consent :
Blessed are the marriages that ne'er repent.

From NATHANIEL FIELD'S *Amends for Ladies*, 1618.

RISE, LADY MISTRESS, RISE!

RISE, lady mistress, rise !
  The night hath tedious been ;
No sleep hath fallen into my eyes,
  Nor slumbers made me sin.
Is not she a saint, then, say,
Thought of whom keeps sin away?

Rise, madam, rise and give me light,
  Whom darkness still will cover,
And ignorance darker than night,
  Till thou shine on thy lover.
All want day till thy beauty rise,
For the grey morn breaks from thine eyes.

> From *Swetnam, the Woman-Hater, arraigned by Women*, 1620.

DING DONG, DONG.

WHILST we sing the doleful knell
    Of this princess' passing-bell,
Let the woods and valleys ring
Echoes to our sorrowing;
And the tenor of their song,
Be ding dong, ding, dong, dong,
    Ding dong, dong,
        Ding, dong.

Nature now shall boast no more
Of the riches of her store,
Since in this her chiefest prize,
All the stock of beauty dies:
Then, what cruel heart can long
Forbear to sing this sad ding dong?
    This sad ding dong,
        Ding dong.

Fauns and sylvans of the woods,
Nymphs that haunt the crystal floods,
Savage beasts more milder then [1]
The unrelenting hearts of men,
Be partakers of our moan,
And with us sing ding dong, ding dong,
    Ding dong, dong,
        Ding dong.

[1] Old form of "than."

From PHILIP MASSINGER'S *The
Emperor of the East*, 1631.

DEATH INVOKED.

WHY art thou slow, thou rest of trouble, Death,
    To stop a wretch's breath,
That calls on thee, and offers her sad heart
    A prey unto thy dart?
I am nor young nor fair; be, therefore, bold:
    Sorrow hath made me old,
Deformed, and wrinkled; all that I can crave
    Is quiet in my grave.
Such as live happy, hold long life a jewel;
    But to me thou art cruel,
If thou end not my tedious misery
    And I soon cease to be.
Strike, and strike home, then; pity unto me,
    In one short hour's delay, is tyranny.

From PHILIP MASSINGER'S *The
Guardian*, 1633.

THE FOREST'S QUEEN.

WELCOME, thrice welcome to this shady green,
    Our long-wished Cynthia, the forest's queen!
The trees begin to bud, the glad birds sing
In winter, changed by her into the spring.
        We know no night,
        Perpetual light
           Dawns from your eye:
        You being near,
        We cannot fear,
           Though death stood by.

From you our swords take edge, our hearts grow bold;
From you in fee their lives your liegemen hold.

These groves your kingdom, and our laws your will;
Smile, and we spare; but if you frown, we kill.
      Bless then the hour
      That gives the power
        In which you may,
      At bed and board,
      Embrace your lord
        Both night and day.
Welcome, thrice welcome to this shady green,
Our long-wished Cynthia, the forest's queen!

From JAMES SHIRLEY'S *The School of Compliments*, 1631.[1]

PAN'S HOLIDAY.

WOODMEN, shepherds, come away,
    This is Pan's great holiday;
      Throw off cares;
With your heaven-aspiring airs
      Help us to sing,
While valleys with your echoes ring.

Nymphs that dwell within these groves
Leave your arbours, bring your loves;
      Gather posies,
Crown your golden hair with roses;
      As you pass,
Foot like fairies on the grass.

Joy crown[2] our bowers! Philomel,
Leave of Tereus' rape to tell.
      Let trees dance,
As they at Thracian lyre did once;
      Mountains play,
This is the shepherds' holiday.

[1] Licensed for the stage 10 February, 1624-5.   [2] Old ed. "drown."

From JAMES SHIRLEY'S *The Witty Fair One*, 1633.[1]

THE FAIR FELON.

IN Love's name you are charged hereby
To make a speedy hue and cry,
After a face, who t'other day,
Came and stole my heart away ;
For your directions in brief
These are best marks to know the thief :
Her hair a net of beams would prove,
Strong enough to captive Jove,
Playing the eagle ; her clear brow
Is a comely field of snow.
A sparkling eye, so pure a gray
As when it shines it needs no day.
Ivory dwelleth on her nose ;
Lilies, married to the rose,
Have made her cheek the nuptial bed ;
Her lips betray their virgin red,
As they only blushed for this,
That they one another kiss.
But observe, beside the rest,
You shall know this felon best
By her tongue ; for if your ear
Shall once a heavenly music hear,
Such as neither gods nor men
But from that voice shall hear again,
That, that is she, oh, take her t'ye,
None can rock heaven asleep but she.

[1] Licensed for the stage in October, 1628.

JAMES SHIRLEY.

SECRECY.

LOVE, a thousand sweets distilling,
  And with nectar bosoms filling,
Charm all eyes that none may find us ;
Be above, before, behind us ;
And, while we thy pleasures taste,
  Enforce time itself to stay,
And by [the] forelock hold him fast
  Lest occasion slip away.

> From JAMES SHIRLEY'S *The Changes, or Love in a Maze*, 1632.

TO CUPID.

IF Love his arrows shoot so fast,
  Soon his feathered stock will waste :
But I mistake in thinking so,
Love's arrows in his quiver grow;
How can he want artillery?
That appears too true in me :
Two shafts feed upon my breast,
Oh make it quiver for the rest !
Kill me with love, thou angry son
Of Cytherea, or let one,
One sharp golden arrow fly
To wound her heart for whom I die.
Cupid, if thou beest a child,
Be no god, or be more mild.

From JAMES SHIRLEY'S *The Bird in a Cage*, 1633.

THE FOOL'S EXCELLENCE.

AMONG all sorts of people,
   The matter if we look well to,
The fool is the best, he from the rest
   Will carry away the bell too.
All places he is free of,
   And foots it without blushing
At masques and plays, is not the bays
   Thrust out, to let the plush in?
Your fool is fine, he's merry,
   And of all men doth fear least,
At every word he jests with my lord,
   And tickles my lady in earnest:
The fool doth pass the guard now,
   He'll kiss his hand, and leg it,
When wise men prate, and forfeit their state,
   Who but the fine fool will beg it?
He without fear can walk in
   The streets that are so stony;
Your gallant sneaks, your merchant breaks,
   He's a fool that does owe no money.

> From JAMES SHIRLEY'S *The Triumph of Peace*, 1633.

THE CLOSE OF THE MASQUE.

COME away, away, away!
  See the dawning of the day,
Risen from the murmuring streams;
Some stars show with sickly beams,
What stock of flame they are allowed,
Each retiring to a cloud;
Bid your active sports adieu,
The morning else will blush for you.
Ye feather-footed hours run
To dress the chariot of the sun;
Harness the steeds, it quickly will
Be time to mount the eastern hill.
The lights grow pale with modest fears,
Lest you offend their sacred ears
And eyes, that lent you all this grace;
Retire, retire, to your own place.
And as you move from that blest pair,
Let each heart kneel, and think a prayer,
That all that can make up the glory
Of good and great may fill their story.

From JAMES SHIRLEY'S *St. Patrick for Ireland*, 1640.

HANG SORROW AND CAST AWAY CARE.

I NEITHER will lend nor borrow,
  Old age will be here to-morrow;
This pleasure we are made for,
When death comes all is paid for:
    No matter what's the bill of fare,
    I'll take my cup, I'll take no care.

Be wise, and say you had warning,
To laugh is better than learning;
To wear no clothes, not neat is;
But hunger is good where meat is:
    Give me wine, give me a wench,
    And let her parrot talk in French.

It is a match worth the making,
To keep the merry-thought waking;
A song is better than fasting,
And sorrow's not worth the tasting:
    Then keep your brain light as you can,
    An ounce of care will kill a man.

From JAMES SHIRLEY'S *The Imposture*, 1652.[1]

PEACE RESTORED.

YOU virgins, that did late despair
   To keep your wealth from cruel men,
Tie up in silk your careless hair:
   Soft peace is come again.

Now lovers' eyes may gently shoot
   A flame that will not kill;
The drum was angry, but the lute
   Shall whisper what you will.

Sing Io, Io! for his sake
   That hath restored your drooping heads;
With choice of sweetest flowers make
   A garden where he treads;

Whilst we whole groves of laurel bring,
   A petty triumph for his brow,
Who is the master of our spring
   And all the bloom we owe.[2]

---

[1] Licensed for the stage in November, 1640.
[2] An old form of "own."

SONG OF NUNS.

O FLY, my soul ! what hangs upon
      Thy drooping wings,
      And weighs them down
With love of gaudy mortal things?

The Sun is now i' the east ; each shade,
      As he doth rise,
      Is shorter made,
That earth may lessen to our eyes.

Oh, be not careless then and play
      Until the star of peace
Hide all his beams in dark recess.
Poor pilgrims needs must lose their way
When all the shadows do increase.

From JAMES SHIRLEY'S *The Cardinal*, 1652.[1]

DAPHNE AND STREPHON.

Strephon. COME, my Daphne, come away,
      We do waste the crystal day ;
 'Tis Strephon calls.
Daphne.   What would my love ?
Strephon. Come, follow to the myrtle grove,
      Where Venus shall prepare
      New chaplets for thy hair.
Daphne. Were I shut up within a tree,
      I'd rend my bark to follow thee.

[1] Licensed for the stage in November, 1641.

Strephon. My shepherdess, make haste,
          The minutes fly too fast.
Daphne. In these cooler shades will I,
          Blind as Cupid, kiss thine eye.
Strephon. In thy perfumed bosom then I'll stray;
          In such warm snow who would not lose his
            way?
Chorus. We'll laugh and leave the world behind;
           And gods themselves that see
            Shall envy thee and me,
              But never find
          Such joys when they embrace a deity.

From JAMES SHIRLEY'S *The
Triumph of Beauty*, 1646.

THE LOVER'S PERPLEXITY.

HEIGH-HO, what shall a shepherd do
    That is in love and cannot woo?
By sad experience now I find
That love is dumb as well as blind.
Her hair is bright, her forehead high;
Then am I taken with her eye.
Her cheeks I must commend for gay,
But then her nose hangs in my way.
Her lips I like, but then steps in
Her white and pretty dimpled chin.
But then her neck I do behold,
Fit to be hanged in chains of gold.
Her breast is soft as any down,
Beneath which lies her maiden town,
So strong and fortified within,
There is no hope to take it in.[1]

[1] "Take in"—capture.

From JAMES SHIRLEY'S *Cupid and Death: A Masque*, 1653.

LOVE'S VICTORIES.

THOUGH little be the god of love,
  Yet his arrows mighty are,
And his victories above
What the valiant reach by war.
Nor are his limits with the sky;
O'er the milky way he'll fly
And sometimes wound a deity.
Apollo once the Python slew,
But a keener arrow flew
From Daphne's eye, and made a wound
For which the god no balsam found.
One smile of Venus, too, did more
On Mars than armies could before.
If a warm fit thus pull him down,
How will she ague-shake him with a frown!
Thus Love can fiery spirits tame,
And, when he please, cold rocks inflame.

DEATH'S SUBTLE WAYS.

VICTORIOUS men of earth, no more
    Proclaim how wide your empires are ;
Though you bind in every shore
    And your triumphs reach as far
        As night or day,
    Yet you, proud monarchs, must obey
And mingle with forgotten ashes when
Death calls ye to the crowd of common men.

Devouring Famine, Plague, and War,
    Each able to undo mankind,
Death's servile emissaries are ;
    Nor to these alone confined,
        He hath at will
    More quaint and subtle ways to kill ;
A smile or kiss, as he will use the art,
Shall have the cunning skill to break a heart.

From JAMES SHIRLEY'S *The Contention of Ajax and Ulysses*, 1659.

NO ARMOUR AGAINST FATE.

THE glories of our blood and state
   Are shadows, not substantial things ;
There is no armour against Fate ;
   Death lays his icy hand on kings :
      Sceptre and crown
      Must tumble down,
And in the dust be equal made
With the poor crooked scythe and spade.

Some men with swords may reap the field,
   And plant fresh laurels where they kill ;
But their strong nerves at last must yield ;
   They tame but one another still :
      Early or late,
      They stoop to fate,
And must give up their murmuring breath,
When they, pale captives, creep to death.

The garlands wither on your brow,
   Then boast no more your mighty deeds ;
Upon Death's purple altar now,
   See where the victor-victim bleeds :
      Your heads must come
      To the cold tomb ;
Only the actions of the just
Smell sweet and blossom in their dust.

From Thomas Randolph's
*Aristippus, or the Jovial
Philosopher*, 1630.

FILL THE CUP AND FILL THE CAN.

SLAVES are they that heap up mountains,
    Still desiring more and more:
Still let's carouse in Bacchus' fountains,
    Never dreaming to be poor.
Give us then a cup of liquor,
    Fill it up unto the brim;
For then (methinks) my wits grow quicker
    When my brains in liquor swim.

OLD SACK IS OUR HEALTH.

WE care not for money, riches or wealth;
    Old sack is our money, old sack is our health.
       Then let's flock hither
       Like birds of a feather,
To drink, to sting,
To laugh and sing,
       Conferring our notes together,
       Conferring our notes together.
Come, let us laugh, let us drink, let us sing;
The winter with us is as good as the spring.
       We care not a feather
       For wind or for weather,
But night and day
We sport and play,
       Conferring our notes together,
       Conferring our notes together.

From SIR JOHN SUCKLING'S
Aglaura, 1638.

WHY SO PALE AND WAN, FOND LOVER.

WHY so pale and wan, fond lover?
    Prithee why so pale?
Will, when looking well can't move her,
    Looking ill prevail?
    Prithee why so pale?

Why so dull and mute, young sinner?
    Prithee why so mute?
Will, when speaking well can't win her,
    Saying nothing do't?
    Prithee why so mute?

Quit, quit, for shame; this will not move,
    This cannot take her;
If of herself she will not love,
    Nothing can make her:
    The devil take her!

TRUE LOVE.

No, no, fair heretic, it needs must be
    But an ill love in me,
      And worse for thee;
For were it in my power
To love thee now this hour
    More than I did the last;
'Twould then so fall,
    I might not love at all;
Love that can flow, and can admit increase,
Admits as well an ebb, and may grow less.

True love is still the same; the torrid zones,
    And those more frigid ones,
      It must not know:
For love grown cold or hot,
    Is lust or friendship, not
      The thing we have.
For that's a flame would die,
Held down or up too high:
Then think I love more than I can express,
And would love more, could I but love thee less.

From Sir John Suckling's
Brennoralt, 1639.

HIS MISTRESS' BEST USE.

She's pretty to walk with:
    And witty to talk with:
And pleasant too to think on.
    But the best use of all
    Is, her health is a stale,[1]
And helps us to make us drink on.

[1] An "excuse for the glass."

DRINKING COMMENDED.

COME let the state stay,
And drink away,
There is no business above it :
It warms the cold brain,
Makes us speak in high strain ;
He's a fool that does not approve it.

The Macedon youth
Left behind him this truth,
That nothing is done with much thinking ;
He drunk, and he fought,
Till he had what he sought ;
The world was his own by good drinking.

From SIR JOHN SUCKLING'S *The Sad One*, 1646.

THE FALSE ONE.

HAST thou seen the down in the air,
When wanton blasts have tossed it?
Or the ship on the sea,
When ruder winds have crossed it?
Hast thou marked the crocodile's weeping,
Or the fox's sleeping?
Or hast thou viewed the peacock in his pride,
Or the dove by his bride,
When he courts for his lechery?
Oh ! so fickle, oh ! so vain, oh ! so false, so false is she !

From WILLIAM CARTWRIGHT'S
The Royal Slave, 1639.

LOVE AND MUSIC.

COME, my sweet, whiles every strain
    Calls our souls into the ear,
Where they greedy listing fain
    Would turn into the sound they hear;
        Lest in desire
        To fill the quire,
        Themselves they tie
        To harmony,
Let's kiss and call them back again.

Now let's orderly convey
    Our souls into each other's breast,
Where interchanged let them stay
    Slumb'ring in a melting rest;
        Then with new fire
        Let them retire,
        And still present
        Sweet fresh content
Youthful as the early day.

Then let us a tumult make,
    Shuffling so our souls that we,
Careless who did give or take,
    May not know in whom they be;
        Then let each smother
        And stifle the other,
        Till we expire
        In gentle fire
Scorning the forgetful lake.

From WILLIAM CARTWRIGHT'S
The Siege, or Love's Convert,
1651.

SEAL UP HER EYES, O SLEEP.

SEAL up her eyes, O sleep, but flow
  Mild as her manners, to and fro;
Slide soft into her, that yet she
May receive no wound from thee.
And ye present her thoughts, O dreams,
With hushing winds and purling streams,
Whiles hovering silence sits without,
Careful to keep disturbance out.
Thus seize her, sleep, thus her again resign;
So what was Heaven's gift we'll reckon thine.

From FRANCIS QUARLES' *The
Virgin Widow*, 1649.

HOW BLEST ARE THEY!

HOW blest are they that waste their weary hours
  In solemn groves and solitary bowers,
Where neither eye nor ear
Can see or hear
The frantic mirth
And false delights of frolic earth;
Where they may sit and pant,
And breathe their pursy souls;
Where neither grief consumes, nor griping want
Afflicts, nor sullen care controls!
Away false joys! ye murder where ye kiss;
There is no heaven to that, no life to this.

From PETER HAUSTED'S *The Rival Friends*, 1632.

A DIALOGUE BETWIXT VENUS, THETIS, AND PHŒBUS.

Venus. DROWSY Phœbus, come away
　　　And let out the longed-for day ;
　　　Leave thy Thetis' silver breast
　　　And ope the casements of the east.
　　　'Tis Venus calls : away, away !
　　　The waking mortals long for day.
Thetis. And let them long ; 'tis just and right
　　　To shut them in eternal night
　　　Whose deeds deserve no day.　Lie still,
　　　Arise not yet, lie still, my Sun ;
　　　My night begins when thou art gone.
Venus. I'll woo thee with a kiss to come away.
Thetis. And I with forty for to stay.
Venus. I'll give to thee the fair Adonis' spear,
　　　So thou wilt rise.
Thetis. 　　　　　　　And I, to keep thee here,
　　　Will give a wreath of pearl as fair
　　　As ever sea-nymph yet did wear.
　　　'Tis Thetis woos thee stay : O stay, O stay !
Venus. 'Tis Venus woos thee rise : O come away !
Phœbus. To which of these shall I mine ear incline?
Venus. Unto the upper world repair.
Thetis. O no, I'll bind him in my flowing hair.
Phœbus. But see fond mortals how they gaze
　　　　On that same petty blaze !
　　　Thetis, adieu, I am no longer thine ;
　　　　I must away, for, if I stay,
　　　My deity's quite undone ;
　　　They will forget t'adore the rising sun.

HAVE PITY, GRIEF.

HAVE pity, Grief; I cannot pay
　　The tribute which I owe thee, tears;
　　　　Alas those fountains are grown dry,
　　　　And 'tis in vain to hope supply
　　From others' eyes; for each man bears
　　　　Enough about him of his own
　　　　To spend his stock of tears upon.

Woo then the heavens, gentle Love,
　　To melt a cloud for my relief,
　　　　Or woo the deep, or woo the grave;
　　　　Woo what thou wilt, so I may have
　　Wherewith to pay my debt, for Grief
　　　　Has vowed, unless I quickly pay,
　　　　To take both life and love away.

TO CUPID.

CUPID, if a God thou art,
　　Transfix this monster's stubborn heart;
But if all thy shafts be flown,
And thy quiver empty grown,
Here be ladies that have eyes
Can furnish thee with new supplies.
　　　Yet, winged archer, do not shoot at all;
　　　'Tis pity that he should so nobly fall.

IN PRAISE OF HIS MISTRESS.

HAVE you a desire to see
    The glorious Heaven's epitome?
Or an abstract of the spring?
Adonis' garden, or a thing
    Fuller of wonder? Nature's shop displayed,
      Hung with the choicest pieces she has made?
        Here behold it open laid.

Or else would you bless your eyes
With a type of paradise?
Or behold how poets feign
Jove to sit amidst his train?
    Or see (what made Actæon rue)
    Diana 'mongst her virgin crew?
      Lift up your eyes and view.

From THOMAS GOFFE'S *The Courageous Turk*, 1632.

DROP GOLDEN SHOWERS, GENTLE SLEEP.

DROP golden showers, gentle sleep;
    And all the angels of the night,
Which do us in protection keep,
Make this queen dream of delight.
Morpheus, be kind a little, and be
Death's now true image, for 'twill prove
To this poor queen that then thou art he.
Her grave is made i' th' bed of love:
Thus with sweet sweets can Heaven mix gall,
And marriage turn to funeral.

From THOMAS GOFFE'S *The Careless Shepherdess*, 1656.

SYLVIA'S BOWER.

COME, shepherds, come, impale your brows
With garlands of the choicest flowers
   The time allows:
Come, nymphs, decked in your dangling hair,
And unto Sylvia's shady bower
   With haste repair;
Where you shall see chaste turtles play,
And nightingales make lasting May,
As if old Time his youthful mind
To one delighted season had confined.

NOW FIE ON LOVE![1]

NOW fie on love! it ill befits,
 Or man and woman know it:
Love was not meant for people in their wits,
 And they that fondly show it
Betray their too much feathered brains,
And shall have only Bedlam for their pains.

To love is to distract my sleep,
 And waking to wear fetters;
To love is but to go to school to weep;
 I'll leave it for my betters.
If single love be such a curse,
To marry is to make it ten times worse.

[1] This song probably belongs to Shirley. See *Notes* at the end.

From *The London Chanticleers.
A Witty Comedy*, 1659.[1]

BRING US IN GOOD ALE.

SUBMIT, bunch of grapes,
    To the strong barley-ear;
The weak vine no longer
    The laurel shall wear:

Sack, and all drinks else,
    Desist from the strife;
Ale's th' only *aqua vitæ*
    And liquor of life.

Then come, my boon fellows,
    Let's drink it around;
It keeps us from th' grave,
    Though it lays us o' th' ground.

Ale's a physician,
    No mountebank bragger,
Can cure the chill ague,
    Though 't be with the stagger.

Ale's a strong wrestler,
    Flings all it hath met,
And makes the ground slippery
    Though 't be not wet.

But come, my boon, &c.

---

[1] Written several years before the date of publication.

Ale is both Ceres
   And good Neptune too;
Ale's froth was the sea
   From whence Venus grew.

Ale is immortal,
   And be there no stops
In bonny lads' quaffing,
   Can live without hops.

Then come, my boon fellows,
   Let's drink it around;
It keeps us from th' grave,
   Though it lays us o' th' ground.

From THOMAS NABBES' *Tottenham Court*, 1638.

THE MILKMAID.

WHAT a dainty life the milkmaid leads,
   When over the flowery meads
She dabbles in the dew
And sings to her cow,
And feels not the pain
Of love or disdain !
She sleeps in the night, though she toils in the day,
And merrily passeth her time away.

From WILLIAM HABINGTON'S
The Queen of Arragon, 1640.

HIS MISTRESS FLOUTED.

FINE young folly, though you were
   That fair beauty I did swear,
  Yet you ne'er could reach my heart:
For we courtiers learn at school,
Only with your sex to fool;
  You're not worth the serious part.

When I sigh and kiss your hand,
Cross my arms and wondering stand,
  Holding parley with your eye,
Then dilate on my desires,
Swear the sun ne'er shot such fires,—
  All is but a handsome lie.

When I eye your curl or lace,
Gentle soul, you think your face
  Straight some murder doth commit;
And your virtue doth begin
To grow scrupulous of my sin,
  When I talk to show my wit.

Therefore, madam, wear no cloud,
Nor to check my love grow proud;
  In sooth I much do doubt,
'Tis the powder in your hair,
Not your breath, perfumes the air,
  And your clothes that set you out.

Yet though truth has this confessed,
And I vow I love in jest,
   When I next begin to court,
And protest an amorous flame,
You will swear I in earnest am:
   Bedlam! this is pretty sport.

From *Corona Minervæ, or a Masque presented before Prince Charles his Highness*, &c., 1635.

WINTER.

COLD Winter brings to crown your age,
[When] many happy years are told,
The myrtle, savory, and sage,
The *semper viva*, never old;
To crown your high victorious brows
Green laurel garlands, arbute boughs,
With palms and olives, whose increase
Are emblems of your lasting peace.
Nor is cold Winter yet at all
Less frolic than the wanton Spring:
The robin redbreast in the hall
Picking up crumbs at Christmas sing;
When winds blow cold and ways be foul,
In barns and sheepcotes sits the owl,
Whose note the husbandman delights
Whenas she hoots in frosty nights.

From AURELIAN TOWNSHEND'S
Albion's Triumph, 1631.

MERCURY COMPLAINING.

Mercury.

WHAT makes me so unnimbly rise,
    That did descend so fleet?
There is no uphill in the skies,
    Clouds stay not feathered feet.

Chorus.

Thy wings are singed, and thou canst fly
But slowly now, swift Mercury.

Mercury.

Some lady here is sure to blame,
    That from Love's starry skies
Hath shot some beam or sent some flame
    Like lightning from her eyes.

Chorus.

Tax not the stars with what the sun,
Too near approached, incensed hath done.

Mercury.

I'll roll me in Aurora's dew
    Or lie in Tethys' bed,
Or from cool Iris beg a few
    Pure opal showers new shed.

Chorus.

Nor dew, nor showers, nor sea can slake
Thy quenchless heat, but Lethe's lake.

From Joseph Rutter's *The Shepherd's Holiday*, 1635.

SONG OF VENUS AND THE GRACES.

COME, Lovely Boy! unto my court,
    And leave these uncouth woods and all
    That feed thy fancy with love's gall
But keep away the honey and the sport!

Chorus of Graces—Come unto me!
        · And with variety
Thou shalt be fed: which Nature loves, and I.

    There is no music in a voice
        That is but one, and still the same:
        Inconstancy is but a name
    To fright poor lovers from a better choice.

Chorus—Come then to me!——

    Orpheus that on Eurydice
        Spent all his love, on others scorn,
        Now on the banks of Hebrus torn
    Finds the reward of foolish constancy.

Chorus—Come then to me!——

    And sigh no more for one love lost!
        I have a thousand Cupids here
        Shall recompense with better cheer
    Thy misspent labours and thy bitter cost.

Chorus—Come then to me!——

PRAISE OF HYMEN.

HYMEN, god of marriage-bed,
    Be thou ever honoured:
Thou, whose torch's purer light
Death's sad tapers did affright,
And instead of funeral fires
Kindled lovers' chaste desires:
      May their love
      Ever prove
True and constant; let not age
Know their youthful heat t'assuage.

Maids, prepare the genial bed:
Then come, night, and hide that red
Which her cheeks, his heart does burn;
Till the envious day return,
And the lusty bridegroom say,
" I have chased her fears away,
      And instead
      Of virginhead,
Given her a greater good,
Perfection and womanhood."

From JOHN JONES' *Adrasta*,
1635.

FATE'S DECREE.

DIE, die, ah die !
We all must die :
'Tis Fate's decree ;
Then ask not why.
When we were framed the Fates consultedly
Did make this law, that all things born should die.
Yet Nature strove,
And did deny
We should be slaves
To Destiny :
At which they heap
Such misery,
That Nature's self
Did wish to die,
And thanked their goodness that they would foresee
To end our cares with such a mild decree.

COME, LOVERS, BRING YOUR CARES.

COME, lovers, bring your cares,
Bring sigh-perfumed sweets,
Bedew the grave with tears,
Where death and virtue meets.
Sigh for the hapless hour
That knit two hearts in one,
And only gave love power
To die when 'twas begun.

> From *Luminalia, or the Festival of Light. Personated in a Masque at Court,* 1637.

THE SONG OF NIGHT.

IN wet and cloudy mists I slowly rise,
   As with mine own dull weight opprest,
To close with sleep the jealous lover's eyes,
   And give forsaken virgins rest.

Th' advent'rous merchant and the mariner,
   Whom storms all day vex in the deep,
Begin to trust the winds when I appear,
   And lose their dangers in their sleep.

The studious that consume their brains and sight
   In search where doubtful knowledge lies,
Grow weary of their fruitless use of light,
   And wish my shades to ease their eyes.

Th' ambitious toiling statesman that prepares
   Great mischiefs ere the daÿ begins,
Not measures day by hours, but by his cares;
   And night must intermit his sins.

Then why, when my slow chariot used to climb,
   Did old mistaking sages weep?
As if my empire did usurp their time,
   And hours were lost when spent in sleep?

I come to ease their labours and prevent
   That weariness which would destroy;
The profit of their toils are still misspent
   Till rest enables to enjoy.

From SAMUEL HARDING'S *Sicily and Naples, or the Fatal Union. A Tragedy*, 1640.

NOBLEST BODIES ARE BUT GILDED CLAY.

Chorus. NOBLEST bodies are but gilded clay:
   Put away
But the precious shining rind,
The inmost rottenness remains behind.
1. Kings, on earth though gods they be,
Yet in death are vile as we;
He, a thousands' king before,
Now is vassal unto more.
2. Vermin now insulting lie,
And dig for diamonds in each eye;
Whilst the sceptre-bearing hand
Cannot their inroads withstand.
3. Here doth one in odours wade
By the regal unction made,
While another dares to gnaw
On that tongue, his people's law.
Chorus. Fools, ah fools, are we, who so contrive,
  And do strive,
In each gaudy ornament,
Who shall his corpse in the best dish present.

From Richard Brome's *Northern Lass*, 1632.

HUMILITY.

Nor Love nor Fate dare I accuse
 For that my love did me refuse,
But oh! mine own unworthiness
That durst presume so mickle bliss.
It was too much for me to love
A man so like the gods above:
An angel's shape, a saint-like voice,
Are too divine for human choice.

Oh had I wisely given my heart
For to have loved him but in part;
Sought only to enjoy his face,
Or any one peculiar grace
Of foot, of hand, of lip, or eye,—
I might have lived where now I die:
But I, presuming all to choose,
Am now condemned all to lose.

From Richard Brome's *A Jovial Crew, or the Merry Beggars*, 1652.

THE MERRY BEGGARS.

COME, come away! the spring,
By every bird that can but sing,
Or chirp a note, doth now invite
Us forth to taste of his delight,
In field, in grove, on hill, in dale;
But above all the nightingale,
Who in her sweetness strives t'outdo
The loudness of the hoarse cuckoo.
 "Cuckoo," cries he; "Jug, jug, jug," sings she;
 From bush to bush, from tree to tree:
 Why in one place then tarry we?

Come away! why do we stay?
We have no debt or rent to pay;
No bargains or accounts to make,
Nor land or lease to let or take:
Or if we had, should that remore us
When all the world's our own before us,
And where we pass and make resort,
It is our kingdom and our court?
 "Cuckoo," cries he, &c.

From WILLIAM STRODE'S *The Floating Island*, 1655.[1]

ADONIS' GOOD-NIGHT.

ONCE Venus' cheeks, that shamed the morn,
    Their hue let fall ;
Her lips, that winter had out-borne,
    In June looked pale.
Her heat grew cold, her nectar dry ;
No juice she had but in her eye
The wonted fire and flames to mortify.
When was this so dismal sight ?
When Adonis bade good-night.

From ROBERT DAVENPORT'S *King John and Matilda*, 1655.[2]

A REQUIEM.

MATILDA, now go take thy bed
    In the dark dwellings of the dead ;

And rise in the great waking day,
Sweet as incense, fresh as May.

Rest thou, chaste soul, fixed in thy proper sphere,
Amongst Heaven's fair ones ; all are fair ones there.

Chorus. Rest there, chaste soul, whilst we here troubled say
    "Time gives us griefs, Death takes our joys away."

---

[1] Acted by the students of Christ Church in 1636.
[2] Written before 1639.

From JOHN MILTON'S *Arcades.
Part of an Entertainment
presented to the Countess
Dowager of Derby at Hare-
field* (1634).

O'ER THE SMOOTH ENAMELLED GREEN.

O'ER the smooth enamelled green,
  Where no print of step hath been,
    Follow me, as I sing
    And touch the warbled string;
  Under the shady roof
  Of branching elm star-proof,
    Follow me.
  I will bring you where she sits,
  Clad in splendour, as befits
    Her deity.
  Such a rural queen
  All Arcadia hath not seen.

NYMPHS AND SHEPHERDS, DANCE NO MORE.

NYMPHS and shepherds, dance no more
    By sandy Ladon's lilied banks;
  On old Lycæus or Cyllene hoar,
    Trip no more in twilight ranks;
  Though Erymanth your loss deplore,
    A better soil shall give ye thanks.
  From the stony Mænalus
  Bring your flocks and live with us;
  Here ye shall have better grace,
  To serve the Lady of this place.
  Though Syrinx your Pan's mistress were,
  Yet Syrinx well might wait on her.
    Such a rural queen
    All Arcadia hath not seen.

From JOHN MILTON'S *Comus*, 1637.[1]

THE REVELS.

Comus. THE star that bids the shepherd fold
 Now the top of heaven doth hold,
And the gilded car of day
His glowing axle doth allay
In the steep Atlantic stream,
And the slope sun his upward beam
Shoots against the dusky pole,
Pacing toward the other goal
Of his chamber in the east.
Meanwhile welcome joy and feast,
Midnight shout and revelry,
Tipsy dance and jollity.
Braid your locks with rosy twine,
Dropping odours, dropping wine.
Rigour now has gone to bed,
And Advice with scrupulous head,
Strict Age and sour Severity,
With their grave saws, in slumber lie.
We, that are of purer fire,
Imitate the starry quire,
Who, in their nightly watchful spheres,
Lead in swift round the months and years.
The sounds and seas, with all their finny drove,
Now to the moon in wavering morrice move;

[1] Presented at Ludlow Castle, 1634.

And, on the tawny sands and shelves,
Trip the pert faeries and the dapper elves.
By dimpled brook and fountain-brim
The wood-nymphs, decked with daisies trim,
Their merry wakes and pastimes keep—
What hath night to do with sleep?
Night hath better sweets to prove;
Venus now wakes, and wakens Love.
Come, let us our rites begin
—'Tis only daylight that makes sin—
Which these dun shades will ne'er report.
  Hail, Goddess of nocturnal sport,
Dark-veiled Cotytto, to whom the secret flame
Of midnight torches burns! mysterious dame,
That ne'er art called but when the dragon-womb
Of Stygian darkness spets her thickest gloom,
And makes one blot of all the air,
Stay thy cloudy ebon chair,
Wherein thou ridest with Hecate, and befriend
Us thy vowed priests, till utmost end
Of all thy dues be done, and none left out;
Ere the blabbing eastern scout,
The nice Morn, on the Indian steep,
From her cabined loophole peep,
And to the tell-tale Sun discry
Our concealed solemnity.
Come, knit hands, and beat the ground
In a light fantastic round!

ECHO INVOKED.

SWEET Echo, sweetest nymph, that livest unseen
  Within thy airy shell
 By slow Meander's margent green,
And in the violet-embroidered vale,
 Where the love-lorn nightingale
Nightly to thee her sad song mourneth well;
Can'st thou not tell me of a gentle pair
 That likest thy Narcissus are?
  Oh! if thou have
 Hid them in some flowery cave
  Tell me but where,
Sweet queen of parley, daughter of the sphere!
So may'st thou be translated to the skies,
And give resounding praise to all heaven's harmonies.

SABRINA.

Spirit. SABRINA fair,
  Listen, where thou art sitting
 Under the glassy, cool, translucent wave,
  In twisted braid of lilies knitting
 The loose train of thy amber-dropping hair;
  Listen for dear honour's sake,
  Goddess of the silver lake,
   Listen, and save!
Listen and appear to us,
In name of great Oceanus,
By the earth-shaking Neptune's mace,
And Tethys' grave majestic pace,
By hoary Nereus' wrinkled look,
And the Carpathian wizard's hook,
By scaly Triton's winding shell,
And old soothsaying Glaucus' spell,
By Leucothea's lovely hands,

And her son that rules the strands,'
By Thetis' tinsel-slippered feet,
And the songs of Sirens sweet,
By dead Parthenope's dear tomb,
And fair Ligeia's golden comb,
Wherewith she sits on diamond-rocks,
Sleeking her soft alluring locks,
By all the nymphs that nightly dance
Upon thy streams with wily glance,
Rise, rise, and heave thy rosy head
From thy coral-paven bed,
And bridle in thy headlong wave,
Till thou our summons answered have.
  Listen, and save!

Sabrina rises, attended by Water-nymphs, and sings.
 By the rushy-fringed bank,
Where grows the willow and the osier dank,
 My sliding chariot stays,
Thick-set with agate, and the azurn sheen
Of turkis blue and emerald green,
 That in the channel strays;
Whilst from off the waters fleet
Thus I set my printless feet
 O'er the cowslip's velvet head,
  That bends not as I tread.
 Gentle swain, at thy request
  I am here.

Spirit. Goddess dear,
 We implore thy powerful hand
 To undo the charmed band
 Of true virgin here distrest,
Through the force, and through the wile
Of unblest enchanter vile.

Sabrina.   Shepherd, 'tis my office best
        To help ensnared chastity.
        Brightest lady, look on me.
        Thus I sprinkle on thy breast
        Drops that from my fountain pure
        I have kept of precious cure,
        Thrice upon thy finger's tip,
        Thrice upon thy rubied lip;
        Next this marble, venomed seat,
        Smeared with gums of glutinous heat,
        I touch with chaste palms moist and cold.
        Now the spell hath lost his hold;
        And I must haste ere morning-hour
        To wait in Amphitrite's bower.

        [*Sabrina descends, and the Lady rises out*
                    of her seat.

Spirit.   Virgin Daughter of Locrine,
        Sprung from old Anchises' line,
        May thy brimmed waves for this
        Their full tribute never miss,
        From a thousand petty rills
        That tumble down the snowy hills;
        Summer drouht or singed air
        Never scorch thy tresses fair,
        Nor wet October's torrent-flood
        Thy molten crystal fill with mud;
        May thy billows roll ashore
        The beryl, and the golden ore;
        May thy lofty head be crowned
        With many a tower and terrace round;
        And, here and there thy banks upon,
        With groves of myrrh and cinnamon.

THE SPIRIT'S DEPARTURE.

TO the ocean now I fly,
And those happy climes that lie
Where day never shuts his eye,
Up in the broad fields of the sky.
There I suck the liquid air,
All amidst the gardens fair
Of Hesperus, and his daughters three
That sing about the golden tree.
Along the crisped shades and bowers
Revels the spruce and jocund Spring;
The Graces, and the rosy-bosomed Hours,
Thither all their bounties bring.
There eternal summer dwells,
And west-winds with musky wing
About the cedarn alleys fling
Nard and cassia's balmy smells.
Iris there with humid bow
Waters the odorous banks, that blow
Flowers of more mingled hue
Than her purfled scarf can shew,
And drenches with Elysian dew
—List, mortals, if your ears be true—
Beds of hyacinth and roses,
Where young Adonis oft reposes,
Waxing well of his deep wound,
In slumber soft; and on the ground
Sadly sits the Assyrian queen.
But far above, in spangled sheen,
Celestial Cupid her famed son advanced
Holds his dear Psyche, sweet entranced
After her wandering labours long,
Till free consent the gods among

Makes her his eternal bride;
And from her fair unspotted side
Two blissful twins are to be born,
Youth and Joy; so Jove hath sworn.

But now my task is smoothly done,
I can fly or I can run
Quickly to the green earth's end,
Where the bowed welkin slow doth bend;
And from thence can soar as soon
To the corners of the moon.

Mortals, that would follow me,
Love Virtue; she alone is free.
She can teach ye how to climb
Higher than the sphery chime;
Or if Virtue feeble were,
Heaven itself would stoop to her.

From RICHARD FLECKNOE'S
Love's Dominion, 1654.

SILENCE INVOKED.

STILL-BORN Silence, thou that art
Floodgate of the deeper heart;
Offspring of a heavenly kind,
Frost o' the mouth and thaw o' the mind;
Secrecy's confident, and he
Who makes religion mystery
Admiration's speaking'st tongue,—
Leave thy desert shades, among
Reverend hermits' hallowed cells,
Where retired'st Devotion dwells:
With thy enthusiasms come,
Seize this maid, and strike her dumb.

From SIR WILLIAM DAVENANT'S
The Cruel Brother, 1630.

WEEP NO MORE FOR WHAT IS PAST.

WEEP no more for what is past,
   For time in motion makes such haste
He hath no leisure to descry
Those errors which he passeth by.
If we consider accident,
   And how repugnant unto sense
It pays desert with bad event,
   We shall disparage Providence.

From SIR WILLIAM DAVENANT'S
The Unfortunate Lovers, 1643.

LOVE'S LOTTERY.

RUN to love's lottery! Run, maids, and rejoice:
   When, drawing your chance, you meet your own
      choice;
And boast that your luck you help with design,
By praying cross-legged to Old Bishop Valentine.
Hark, hark! a prize is drawn, and trumpets sound!
      Tan, ta, ra, ra, ra!
      Tan, ta, ra, ra, ra!

Hark, maids! more lots are drawn! prizes abound.
Dub! dub a, dub a, dub! the drum now beats!
And, dub a, dub a, dub, echo repeats;
As if at night the god of war had made
Love's queen a skirmish for a serenade.
   Haste, haste, fair maids, and come away!
   The priest attends, your bridegrooms stay.

Roses and pinks will be strewn where you go;
Whilst I walk in shades of willow, willow.
    When I am dead let him that did slay me
    Be but so good as kindly to lay me
    There where neglected lovers mourn,
    Where lamps and hallowed tapers burn,
    Where clerks in quires sad dirges sing,
    Where sweetly bells at burials ring.

      My rose of youth is gone
      Withered as soon as blown!
      Lovers go ring my knell!
      Beauty and love farewell!
      And lest virgins forsaken
      Should, perhaps, be mistaken
In seeking my grave, alas! let them know
I lie near a shade of willow, willow.

THE COQUET.

'TIS, in good truth, a most wonderful thing
   (I am even ashamed to relate it)
That love so many vexations should bring,
   And yet few have the wit to hate it.

Love's weather in maids should seldom hold fair
   Like April's mine shall quickly alter;
I'll give him to-night a lock of my hair,
   To whom next day I'll send a halter.

I cannot abide these malapert males,
   Pirates of love, who know no duty;
Yet love with a storm can take down their sails,
   And they must strike to Admiral Beauty.

Farewell to that maid who will be undone,
   Who in markets of men (where plenty
Is cried up and down) will die even for one;
   I will live to make fools of twenty.

From Sir William Davenant's
The Siege of Rhodes, 1656.

LADIES IN ARMS.

LET us live, live! for, being dead,
    The pretty spots,
Ribbons and knots,
And the fine French dress for the head,
No lady wears upon her
In the cold, cold bed of honour.
Beat down our grottos, and hew down our bowers,
Dig up our arbours, and root up our flowers;
Our gardens are bulwarks and bastions become;
Then hang up our lute, we must sing to the drum.

    Our patches and our curls,
      So exact in each station,
    Our powders and our purls,[1]
      Are now out of fashion.
Hence with our needles, and give us your spades;
We, that were ladies, grow coarse as our maids.
Our coaches have driven us to balls at the court,
We now must drive barrows to earth up the fort.

CURSED JEALOUSY.

THIS cursed jealousy, what is't?
    'Tis love that has lost itself in a mist;
'Tis love being frighted out of his wits;
'Tis love that has a fever got;
Love that is violently hot,
But troubled with cold and trembling fits.
'Tis yet a more unnatural evil:
    Tis the god of love, 'tis the god of love, possessed
      with a devil.

[1] Embroidered borders of lace.

'Tis rich corrupted wine of love,
Which sharpest vinegar does prove ;
From all the sweet flowers which might honey make,
It does a deadly poison bring:
Strange serpent which itself doth sting!
It never can sleep, and dreams still awake ;
It stuffs up the marriage-bed with thorns.
It gores itself, it gores itself, with imagined horns.

From SIR WILLIAM DAVENANT'S
The Man's the Master, 1669.

DRINK, DRINK, DRINK!

THE bread is all baked,
    The embers are raked ;
'Tis midnight now by chanticleer's first crowing ;
    Let's kindly carouse
    Whilst 'top of the house
The cats fall out in the heat of their wooing.
    Time, whilst thy hour-glass does run out,
    This flowing glass shall go about.
Stay, stay, the nurse is waked, the child does cry,
No song so ancient is as lulla-by.
The cradle's rocked, the child is hushed again,
Then hey for the maids, and ho for the men.
    Now everyone advance his glass ;
    Then all at once together clash ;
        Experienced lovers know
        This clashing does but show
That, as in music, so in love must be
Some discord to make up a harmony.
Sing, sing ! When crickets sing why should not we ?

The crickets were merry before us;
They sung us thanks ere we made them a fire.
 They taught us to sing in a chorus:
The chimney's their church, the oven their quire.
Once more the cock cries cock-a-doodle-doo!
The owl cries o'er the barn, to-whit-to-whoo!
Benighted travellers now lose their way
 Whom Will-of-the-wisp bewitches:
About and about he leads them astray
 Through bogs, through hedges, and ditches.
Hark! hark! the cloister bell is rung!
Alas! the midnight dirge is sung.
  Let 'em ring,
  Let 'em sing,
Whilst we spend the night in love and in laughter.
  When night is gone,
  O then too soon
The discords and cares of the day come after.

Come, boys! a health, a health, a double health
To those who 'scape from care by shunning wealth.
  Dispatch it away
  Before it be day,
'Twill quickly grow early when it is late:
  A health to thee,
  To him, to me,
To all who beauty love, and business hate!

From SIR WILLIAM DAVENANT'S
The Law against Lovers, 1673.

WAKE ALL THE DEAD! WHAT HO! WHAT HO!

WAKE all the dead! what ho! what ho!
How soundly they sleep whose pillows lie low?
They mind not poor lovers who walk above
On the decks of the world in storms of love.
   No whisper now nor glance shall pass
   Through wickets or through panes of glass;
For our windows and doors are shut and barred.
Lie close in the church, and in the churchyard.
   In every grave make room, make room!
   The world's at an end, and we come, we come.

The state is now love's foe, love's foe;
'T has seized on his arms, his quiver and bow;
Has pinioned his wings, and fettered his feet,
Because he made way for lovers to meet.
   But, O sad chance, his judge was old;
   Hearts cruel grow, when blood grows cold.
No man being young his process would draw.
O heavens, that love should be subject to law!
   Lovers go woo the dead, the dead!
   Lie two in a grave, and to bed, to bed!

From Sir William Berkley's
The Lost Lady, 1639.

WHERE DID YOU BORROW THAT LAST SIGH?

WHERE did you borrow that last sigh,
   And that relenting groan?
For those that sigh, and not for love,
   Usurp what's not their own.
Love's arrows sooner armour pierce
   Than your soft snowy skin;
Your eyes can only teach us love,
   But cannot take it in.

From Jasper Mayne's *The Amorous War*, 1648.

TIME is the feathered thing,
   And, whilst I praise
The sparklings of thy looks and call them rays,
   Takes wing,
Leaving behind him as he flies
An unperceived dimness in thine eyes.
   His minutes whilst th' are told
     Do make us old;
And every sand of his fleet glass,
Increasing age as it doth pass,
Insensibly sows wrinkles there
Where flowers and roses do appear.
   Whilst we do speak, our fire
     Doth into ice expire;

JASPER·MAYNE.

    Flames turn to frost
     And ere we can
  Know how our crow turns swan,
  Or how a silver snow
   Springs there where jet did grow,
Our fading spring is in dull winter lost.

  Since then the night hath hurled
    Darkness, love's shade,
Over its enemy the day, and made
      The world
  Just such a blind and shapeless thing
As 'twas before light did from darkness spring,
  Let us employ its treasure
    And make shade pleasure;
  Let's number out the hours by blisses,
  And count the minutes by our kisses;
  Let the heavens new motions feel
  And by our embraces wheel.
    And whilst we try the way
    By which love doth convey
     · Soul into soul,
     And mingling so
  Makes them such raptures know
  As makes them entranced lie
  In mutual ecstacy,
Let the harmonious spheres in music roll.

THOMAS FORDE.

From Thomas Forde's *Love's Labyrinth*, 1660.

LOVE'S DUEL.

CUPID all his arts did prove
To invite my heart to love;
But I always did delay
His mild summons to obey,
Being deaf to all his charms.
Straight the god assumes his arms;
With his bow and quiver he
Takes the field to duel me.
Armed like Achilles, I
With my shield alone defy
His bold challenge as he cast
His golden darts, I as fast
Catched his arrows in my shield
Till I made him leave the field.
Fretting and disarmed then
The angry god returns again
All in flames; 'stead of a dart
Throws himself into my heart.
Useless I my shield require
When the fort is all on fire;
I in vain the field did win
Now the enemy's within.
Thus betrayed, at last I cry,
"Love, thou hast the victory."

THE BUSY MAN IS FREE.

FOND Love, no more
Will I adore
Thy feigned Deity;
Go throw thy darts
At simple hearts,
And prove thy victory.

Whilst I do keep
My harmless sheep
Love hath no power on me.
'Tis idle souls
Which he controls;
The busy man is free.

NOTES.

NOTES.

Page 16. "His golden locks time hath to silver turned," &c.—Thackeray quoted the opening lines of this beautiful song in *The Newcomes*.
"His helmet now shall make a hive for bees."—In Alciati's *Emblems* there is an engraving of bees swarming in a helmet. Cf. Geoffrey Whitney's *Choice of Emblems*, 1586 :—

> "The helmet strong that did the head defend,
> Behold, for hive the bees in quiet served;
> And when that wars with bloody blows had end,
> They honey wrought where soldier was preserved :
>   Which doth declare the blessed fruits of peace,
>   How sweet she is when mortal wars do cease."

Page 18. "What thing is love?"—The first six lines are found in an old play, *The Wisdom of Dr. Dodypol*, 1600.

Page 20. "And you shall have some cockell-bread."—Aubrey says that "young wenches have a wanton sport which they call moulding of cockle bread;" and he describes the curious custom.

Page 24. "Autumn hath all the summer's fruitful treasure."—Nashe's play was acted in the autumn of 1593, when the plague was raging. "This low-built house" is Archbishop Whitgift's palace at Croydon. See Dr. Grosart's edition of Nashe's *Works*, vol. vi. pp. xxvi-xxxix.

Page 48. "Take, O, take those lips away."—In Fletcher's *The Bloody Brother*, first printed in 1639, we have this song with the following additional stanza :—

> "Hide, oh, hide those hills of snow,
> Which thy frozen bosom bears,
> On whose tops the pinks that grow
> Are of those that April wears!
> But first set my poor heart free,
> Bound in those icy chains by thee."

The second stanza is distinctly inferior to the first. I take the first to be by Shakespeare and the second by Fletcher.

Page 53. "Plumpy Bacchus with *pink eyne*," *i.e.* with small winking eyes.

Page 61. "Ev'n his face begetteth laughter."—*Laughter* rhymes awkwardly with *slaughter*. Marston alludes to this passage in *The Fawn*, iv. 1 :—"another has vow'd to get the consumption of the lungs or to leave to posterity the true orthography and pronunciation of laughing."

Page 66. "Still to be neat, still to be drest."—This song is modelled on some Latin verses of Jean Bonnefons, "Semper munditias, semper, Basilissa, decores," &c.

Page 69. "Have you seen but a bright lily grow?"—This stanza is imitated by Suckling in his little song beginning :—

> "Hast thou seen the down in the air,
> When wanton blasts have tossed it?"

Page 94. — "'Hey for our town!' cried."—On May-day it was the custom for one village to contend with another in dancing-matches. *Hey for our town!* was the cry raised on such occasions. Cf. *Lyrics from Elizabethan Song-books*, ed. 1887, p. 68:—

> "Then all at once *for our town* cries!
> Pipe on, for we will have the prize."

"To Hogsdon or to Newington."—Hogsdon and Newington were favourite resorts of pleasure-seekers, particularly 'prentices and their sweethearts. They were noted for cakes and cream:—

> "For Hogsdon, Islington, and Tot'nam Court;
> For cakes and cream had then no small resort." (*Wither.*)

Page 133. "Hence, all you vain delights."—This beautiful song undoubtedly gave Milton some hints for *Il Penseroso*. Dr. William Strode, a canon of Christ Church, wrote a reply to Fletcher's verses. It is printed in *Wit Restored*, 1658:—

> "Return, my joys, and hither bring
> A tongue not made to speak but sing,
> A jolly spleen, an inward feast,
> A causeless laugh without a jest;
> A face which gladness doth anoint,
> An arm for joy flung out of joint," &c.

Strode died in 1644; his poems are scattered about the MS. commonplace books and printed miscellanies of the time.

Page 163. "O for a bowl of fat canary."—This song is found (with some variations) in Lyly's *Alexander and Campaspe*, ed. 1632.

Page 166. "Come away, come away."—In my Introduction to Middleton's *Works*, vol. i. p. liv., &c., I have said my say about the relationship between *The Witch* and *Macbeth*.

Page 169. "The hour of sweety night," &c.—Marston's claim to *The Mountebank's Masque* is very shadowy. I have a strong suspicion that this song is by Campion.

Page 174. "Oh, sorrow, sorrow," &c.—*The Noble Spanish Soldier* bears Samuel Rowley's initials on the title-page of the old edition; but there are good reasons for ascribing it—in whole or part—to Dekker. It was entered on the Stationers' Register as a work of Dekker in May 1631, and again in December 1633.

Page 176. "*Swetnam, the Woman-Hater, arraigned by Women*."—A certain Joseph Swetnam (Phœbus, what a name!) published in 1615 a work entitled *The arraignment of lewd, idle, froward and unconstant women, &c.*, which passed through several editions. In the play he is held up to well-merited execration.

Page 186. "Heigh-ho, what shall a shepherd do?"—These verses are found (with some variations) in Thomas Goffe's play *The Careless Shepherdess*, 1656; but they doubtless belong to Shirley.

Page 195. "How blest are they."—This little song of Quarles found its way into Richard Brome's play *The Queen and the Concubine*, printed in 1659.

Page 196. "*The Rival Friends*."—This play was acted before the King and Queen at Cambridge in March 1631. According to the title-page, it was "cried down by Boys, Faction, Envy, and confident Ignorance, approved by the judicious." Peter Hausted, a native of Oundle, belonged to Queen's College, Cambridge. On leaving the University he took orders; and at the outbreak of the Civil War he became chaplain to the Earl of Northampton. He died at Banbury in 1645. *The Rival Friends* is the only play that he wrote in English; but he also published a Latin comedy *Senile Odium*, 1633.

Page 198. "*The Couragious Turke.*"—Thomas Goffe's plays were posthumously published. He was born in 1592, educated at Westminster and at Christ Church, received a living in Surrey, married a shrewish widow (who is said to have made his life miserable), and died in 1627. There is a deal of fustian in his tragedies, but he was genuinely inspired at times.

Page 199. "Now fie on love, it ill befits."—Among Shirley's *Poems*, 1646, we have a shortened form of this song:—

> "Now fie on foolish love! it not befits
>   Or man or woman know it:
> Love was not meant for people in their wits,
>   And they that fondly show it
> Betray the straw and feathers in their brain,
>   And shall have Bedlam for their pain,
>   If single love be such a curse,
>   To marry is to make it ten times worse."

We have seen that another song —"Heigh-ho what shall a shepherd do?"—is ascribed both to Shirley and to Goffe. Shirley claimed them in 1646; and I suspect that they were introduced into Goffe's *Careless Shepherdess*, 1656, by some irresponsible editor.

Page 203. "When winds blow cold and ways be foul,
    In barns and sheepcotes sits the owl."—

We are reminded of Shakespeare's :—

> "When blood is nipped *and ways be foul*,
> Then nightly sings the staring owl."

Page 205. "And leave these *uncouth* woods."— *Uncouth* has the meaning *unfrequented, solitary*.

Page 220. "Still-born Silence, thou that art."— Richard Flecknoe, the author of this beautiful invocation, was immortalized by Dryden. Langbaine writes with mischievous pleasantry :—"He has published sundry works (as he styles them) to continue his name to posterity; tho' possibly an enemy has done that for him which his own endeavours would never have perfected : for whatever become of his own pieces his name will continue whilst Mr. Dryden's satire called *Mac Flecknoe* shall remain in vogue." There is not much to be said in favour of Flecknoe's plays, but some of his poems have real merit. He had been a traveller in Spain, Brazil, and other countries. Southey has a kindly notice of him in *Omniana*, i. 105-10.

Page 221. "Run to love's lottery."—This song and the next are not found in the early editions but first appeared in the folio of 1673.

Page 230. "Love's Duel."—This is a free rendering of the fourteenth ode of Anacreon.

LIST OF AUTHORS.

BEAUMONT, FRANCIS (1586—1616). Pages 89-90.
BEAUMONT, FRANCIS, and FLETCHER, JOHN (1579—1625). 90-100.
BELCHIER, DABRIDGECOURT (d. 1621). 170-1.
BERKLEY, SIR WILLIAM (d. 1677). 228.
BROME, RICHARD (d. 1652?). 210-11.
BROWNE, WILLIAM (1590—1650?). 172.
CAMPION, DR. THOMAS (d. 1620). 88.
CARTWRIGHT, WILLIAM (d. 1643). 194-5.
Corona Minervæ, 1635 (*Anonymous*). 203.
DANIEL, SAMUEL (1562—1619). 75-6.
DAVENANT, SIR WILLIAM (1605—1668). 221-7.
DAVENPORT, ROBERT (fl. 1639). 212.
DEKKER, THOMAS (1570?—1641?). 77-86.
FIELD, NATHANIEL (d. 1633). 175.
FLECKNOE, RICHARD (fl. 1654). 220.
FLETCHER, JOHN. 101-138. *See* also BEAUMONT, FRANCIS.
FLETCHER, JOHN, and ROWLEY, WILLIAM (?—?). 139.
FLETCHER, JOHN, and SHAKESPEARE, WILLIAM (1564—1616). 140-1.
FLETCHER, PHINEAS (d. 1649). 173-4.

FORD, JOHN (1586—?). 144.
FORDE, THOMAS (fl. 1660). 230-1.
GOFFE, THOMAS (1592-1627).' 198-200.
GREENE, ROBERT. *See* LODGE, THOMAS.
HABINGTON, WILLIAM (1605-45). 202-3.
HARDING, SAMUEL (fl. 1640). 209.
HAUSTED, PETER (d. 1645). 196-8.
HEYWOOD, THOMAS (?—?). 145-151.
JONES, JOHN (fl. 1635). 207.
JONSON, BEN (1573-1637). 57-74.
LODGE, THOMAS (d. 1625), and GREENE, ROBERT (1560-92). 21.
London Chanticleers, 1659 (*Anonymous*). 200-1.
Luminalia, or The Festival of Light, 1637 (*Anonymous*). 208.
LYLY, JOHN (1553?—?). 1-12.
MARSTON, JOHN (1575?—1634). 169.
MASSINGER, PHILIP (1584-1639). 177.
MAYNE, JASPER (1604—1672). 228-9.
MIDDLETON, THOMAS (1570?—1627). 162-8.
MIDDLETON, THOMAS, and ROWLEY, WILLIAM. 158-62.
MILTON, JOHN (1608—1674). 213-220.
MUNDAY, ANTHONY (1553—1633). 86-7.
NABBES, THOMAS (fl. 1638). 201.
NASHE, THOMAS (1567—1600?). 22-6.
PEELE, GEORGE (1558?—1598). 13-20.
QUARLES, FRANCIS (1592—1644). 195.
RANDOLPH, THOMAS (1605—1635). 190.
ROWLEY, SAMUEL (?—?). 174.
ROWLEY, WILLIAM. 151-157. *See* also FLETCHER, JOHN ; MIDDLETON, THOMAS.
RUTTER, JOSEPH (fl. 1635). 205-6.

SHAKESPEARE, WILLIAM. 27-56. *See* also FLETCHER, JOHN.
SHIRLEY, JAMES (1594—1666). 178-189.
STRODE, DR. WILLIAM (1599—1644). 211.
SUCKLING, SIR JOHN (1608—1642). 191-3.
Swetnam, the Woman Hater, 1620 (*Anonymous*). 176.
TOWNSHEND, AURELIAN (fl. 1631). 204.
WEBSTER, JOHN (?—?). 142-3.

CHISWICK PRESS:—C. WHITTINGHAM AND CO., TOOKS COURT, CHANCERY LANE.

www.ingramcontent.com/pod-product-compliance
Lightning Source LLC
Chambersburg PA
CBHW031957230426
43672CB00010B/2190